PagePlus X5
Resource Guide

How to contact us

Web:

Serif Website:	http://www.serif.com
Forums:	http://www.serif.com/forums.asp

Main office (UK, Europe):

The Software Centre, PO Box 2000, Nottingham, NG11 7GW, UK

Main:	(0115) 914 2000
Registration (UK only):	(0800) 376 1989
Sales (UK only):	(0800) 376 7070
Customer Service/ Technical Support:	http://www.support.serif.com/
General Fax:	(0115) 914 2020

North American office (US, Canada):

Serif Inc, The Software Center, 17 Hampshire Drive, Suites 1 & 2, Hudson, NH 03051, USA

Main:	(603) 889-8650
Registration:	(800) 794-6876
Sales:	(800) 489 6703
Customer Service/ Technical Support:	http://www.support.serif.com/
General Fax:	(603) 889-1127

International:

Please contact your local distributor/dealer. For further details, please contact us at one of our phone numbers above.

Credits

This Resource Guide, and the software described in it, is furnished under an end user License Agreement, which is included with the product. The agreement specifies the permitted and prohibited uses.

Trademarks

Serif is a registered trademark of Serif (Europe) Ltd.

PagePlus is a registered trademark of Serif (Europe) Ltd.

All Serif product names are trademarks of Serif (Europe) Ltd.

Microsoft, Windows, and the Windows logo are registered trademarks of Microsoft Corporation. All other trademarks acknowledged.

Windows Vista and the Windows Vista Start button are trademarks or registered trademarks of Microsoft Corporation in the United States and/or other countries.

Copyrights

Digital Images ©2008 Hemera Technologies Inc. All Rights Reserved.

Digital Images ©2008 Jupiterimages Corporation, All Rights Reserved.

Digital Images ©2008 Jupiterimages France SAS, All Rights Reserved.

Bitstream Font content © 1981-2005 Bitstream Inc. All rights reserved.

Portions images © 1997-2002 Nova Development Corporation; © 1995 Expressions Computer Software; © 1996-98 CreatiCom, In.; 1996 Cliptoart; © 1997 Multimedia Agency Corporation; © 1997-98 Seattle Support Group. Rights of all parties reserved.

Portions graphics import/export technology © AccuSoft Corp. & Eastman Kodak Company & LEAD Technologies, Inc.

Panose Typeface Matching System ©1991, 1992, 1995-97 Hewlett-Packard Corporation.

THE PROXIMITY HYPHENATION SYSTEM © 1989 Proximity Technology Inc. All rights reserved.

THE PROXIMITY/COLLINS DATABASE © 1990 William Collins Sons & Co. Ltd.; © 1990 Proximity Technology Inc. All rights reserved.

THE PROXIMITY/MERRIAM-WEBSTER DATABASE® © 1990 Merriam-Webster Inc.; © 1990 Proximity Technology Inc. All rights reserved.

The Sentry Spelling-Checker Engine © 2000 Wintertree Software Inc.

The ThesDB Thesaurus Engine © 1993-97 Wintertree Software Inc.

WGrammar Grammar-Checker Engine © 1998 Wintertree Software Inc.

Extensible Metadata Platform (XMP) Copyright © 2006 Adobe Systems Incorporated. All rights reserved.

ICC Colour Profiles © 2006 Adobe Systems Incorporated. All rights reserved.

Introduction

Welcome to the PagePlus X5 Resource Guide! Whether you are new to PagePlus or a seasoned desktop publisher, this guide offers content to help you get the best out of PagePlus.

From a range of illustrated tutorials to get you started or help you accomplish a complex project, to full-colour previews of the theme layouts and Pro Template Packs, we hope you'll find this Resource Guide to be a valuable resource that you'll return to time and time again.

The Resource Guide is organized into the following chapters:

1: Tutorials

Illustrated, step-by-step training covering the basics of PagePlus and desktop publishing.

2: Theme Layouts

Full-colour page previews of the theme layout sets included on the PagePlus X5 Program DVD.

3: Pro Template Packs

A reference gallery of the Pro Template Packs included with PagePlus X5.

Contents

Tutorials

These PagePlus tutorials provide illustrated, step-by-step instructions to show you how to get the best out of desktop publishing.

Throughout each tutorial, you can apply these techniques to your own documents or use the samples available either in PagePlus or online (see individual tutorials for details).

Accessing the tutorials

You can access the tutorials in one of the following ways:

- From the PagePlus Startup Wizard, select from the **Learn** section. Different icons indicate the type of tutorial available.

 a video tutorial

 an online tutorial

 see more tutorials and videos!

- or -

- From PagePlus, click **Help** and then click **Tutorials**.

Accessing the sample files

Throughout the tutorials, you'll be prompted to access sample files. All samples are accessible via the Internet at the following location:

http://go.serif.com/resources/PPX5

If you've clicked on a file, you can either open or save the file. We recommend you save the file to your desktop or a named folder on your computer.

Quick Start

PagePlus provides a wide range of professionally designed theme layouts, which you can use as starting points for your own publications, adding your own pictures and text.

In this tutorial, we'll show you just how easy it is to create an eye-catching, professional-looking document using a theme layout template.

By the end of this tutorial you will be able to:

- Open a **Theme Layout** template.

- Update **User Details**.

- Edit and format text.

- Add and adjust images.

- Change your colour scheme.

Let's begin...

1.   On the **File** menu, click **New > New from Startup Wizard**.

2.   In the **Create** section, click **Use Design Template**.

3.   In the dialog:

- In the **Theme Layouts** list on the left, click the **Illustrative** category, then click **Spiro**.

- In the centre pane, click to select the **Newsletter** thumbnail.

- In the top-right drop-down list, you can choose from three specially designed publication schemes, or any of the colour schemes included with PagePlus. We selected **Scheme 1**.

- In the **Pages** pane, click the check boxes to select the pages that you want to use in your publication—we selected the first two pages.

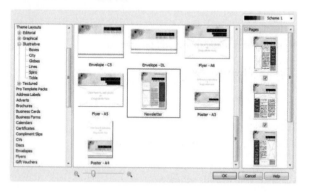

- Click **OK**.

The theme layout opens in the workspace.

User Details

When you create a publication from a theme layout, you'll be prompted to update your **User Details**. These details are stored so that you only need to update them once. Let's do this now.

To update User Details:

1. On the **Business** tab, complete the details required. (We've created a fictional company and address—you can use your own if you want to.)

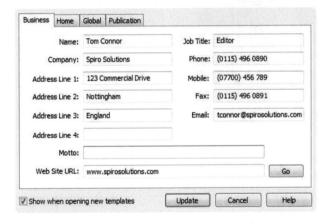

2. Click **Update**.

The publication updates with the new details.

3.   To change the details, click  **Set User Details** and make your changes in the dialog.

Page 1 opens in the workspace and you can see both pages displayed on the **Pages** tab.

To switch between pages:

- In the **Pages** tab, double-click on the page 2 thumbnail to display the page in the workspace.

At the bottom-left of page 2, you can see that the user details have also been updated with the information that you've just entered. However, in our example the email address wraps onto the next line (if you've used a shorter email address, yours may well fit onto a single line). Let's amend this by resizing the text frame. We'll amend this on page 1 to begin with.

- In the **Pages** tab, double-click on the page 1 thumbnail.

To change font size:

1. Click inside the frame, to the left of the word SPIRO and drag to highlight all of the text in the frame.

2. On the Text context toolbar, in the size drop-down list, set the font size to 8 pt.

Notice that our text still doesn't quite fit. If we make the font any smaller, it could make the text hard to read. Instead, we'll resize the text frame so that it fits the text.

To resize and centre a text frame:

1. Click on the border of the text frame to select it. The selected border changes to match the layer colour (in our case blue).

2. Click on the centre-left handle and drag it to the left to increase the width of the text frame until the text fits onto a single line.

3. With the  **Pointer Tool**, click and drag a selection marquee around both the rectangle and the text frame (as illustrated). On release, this selects both objects.

4. On the **Align** tab, select **Relative to: Selection** and then, click  **Centre Vertically** and  **Centre Horizontally**.

The objects are perfectly aligned.

Adding images

The themed layouts provide placeholder picture frames for you to add your own photos. We'll do this now.

To add images:

1. On the **Pages** tab, double-click on page I to display it in the workspace.

2. Click inside the first empty frame. The **Import Picture** dialog opens. Navigate to the picture that you want to use, click to select it, and then click **Open**.

 When you add a picture, you may get a colour profile warning. If this is the case, click **Yes** to normalize the image.

3.   The picture is placed in the frame and the picture frame toolbar
displays beneath it.

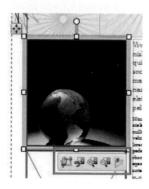

You can use this to adjust your picture inside its frame. We'll try this
now.

To pan an image:

1.   Click the [image] **Pan** tool.

2.   Click and drag the image with the [image] cursor.

3.   Release the mouse button when you are happy with the position of
the image.

We can use the same toolbar to adjust the zoom of the image within the frame.

To adjust zoom level of an image:

- Click the ⊞ **Zoom In** button to zoom in.

- Click the ⊞ **Zoom Out** button to zoom out.

Let's add an image to the other empty picture frames. This time we'll use the **Media Bar**.

To add images with the Media Bar:

1. At the bottom of the workspace, you'll find the **Media Bar**. (If you can't see the **Media Bar**, click the ▬◢▬ handle to open it.)

2. In the drop-down list, select the **PagePlus X5 Tutorial Images** album.

> You can also add images to the **Temporary Album** or create new, permanent albums for frequently used images. For more information on how to do this, see the **How To** tab or PagePlus Help. For more about images in general, take a look at the *Pictures* tutorial (on p. 53).

3. Scroll to the image you want to add (or search for it in the search bar).

4. Drag the thumbnail onto the picture frame.

The image is added to the frame. In the **Media Bar**, a green check mark appears next to the image thumbnail to indicate that it is in use.

5. On the **Pages** tab, double-click the page 2 thumbnail and repeat steps 3 and 4 to add an image to the empty frame.

Let's now have a go at editing some text.

*   On the **Pages** tab, double-click on Page 1.

To edit text:

1.   Click and drag to select the text 'SAPIEN VITAE?'.

2.   Type 'SPIRO SOLUTIONS'.

The original text is replaced but the current formatting is retained.

3.   Triple-click to select the second title line.

4. Type 'NEWSLETTER'.

Once again, the original formatting is retained.

You may also want to change the appearance of your text. Let's demonstrate this now.

To format text:

1. Select the text 'NEWSLETTER'.

2. On the Text context toolbar, in the font drop-down list, select a different font. We chose **Egyptian710 BT**.

3. On the **Swatches** tab, ensure that **Text** is selected and then, click the **Scheme Colour 2** swatch. The text is updated.

You can use any colour swatch to colour your text. However, by using a scheme colour, the text will update to match the colour scheme applied.

To conclude this tutorial, let's change the colour scheme to one that better suits our seasonal publication.

To change the colour scheme:

1. At the bottom-right of the studio, click **Schemes** to expand the **Schemes** tab.

2. On the **Schemes** tab, click to select **Scheme 2**.

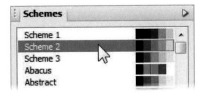

All schemed objects within the publication update with the new colours.

That concludes this tutorial. You should now be feeling familiar with the tools and techniques required to turn a theme layout into your own custom publication.

See the following tutorials for more detailed information on working with text (p. 19, p. 41), pictures (p. 53), and colour schemes (p. 143, p. 153).

Frame Text

This tutorial shows how to create and manipulate frame text. We'll be working with one of the theme layouts included with PagePlus.

By the end of this tutorial you will be able to:

- Create, edit, and format text frames and text.

- Create placeholder text.

- Link text between frames.

- Use layout guides.

- Change scheme colours.

Let's begin...

1. On the **File** menu, click **New > New from Startup Wizard**.

2. In the **Create** section, click **Use Design Template**.

3. In the dialog:

- In the **Theme Layouts** list on the left, click the **Illustrative** category, then click **Spiro**.

- In the centre pane, select the **Newsletter** template.

- In the **Pages** pane, select pages 2, 3 and 4, then clear the page 1 option.

- Click **OK**.

4. In the **User Details** dialog click **Update**. The template opens as a new, three page document in the workspace. Each page is displayed in the **Pages** tab.

About frame text

PagePlus provides two types of text—*frame text* and *artistic text*. Frame text is placed on the page inside a *text frame*, and is generally used for body copy and longer passages of text, or non-decorative text such as contact details, product information, etc.

Artistic text is most often used for titles and decorative text. For more on artistic text, see the *Artistic Text* tutorial.

Frame text has several special properties. It enables you to:

- Flow text between linked frames.

- Wrap text around pictures and shapes.

- Shape the frame to page objects.

Many of the methods described in the following sections, such as selecting and editing text, are applicable to both artistic and frame text. However, in this tutorial, we will concentrate on frame text.

To begin, we'll show you how to select, edit, and format text.

To select and edit text:

1. Click on the title 'HABITASSE' at the top of the page. The Hintline toolbar tells you that this is a *text frame*.

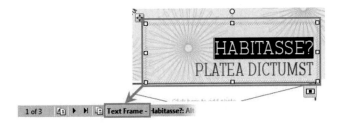

2.   Click to place an insertion point before the 'H' and then drag to the right to select the entire top line of text.

3.   Type 'SPIRO SOLUTIONS'.

4.   Triple-click on the second line of text to select it.

5.   Type 'WINTER'.

Well done, the title is complete and you've now used two methods to select text! Let's move on to look at some of the ways we can edit a text frame.

Linked frames

In PagePlus, you can link multiple text frames. This allows the text to flow from one frame to another automatically. If a frame is linked, when selected, a 🖃 **Link** button displays at the bottom right of the frame. When you delete a linked frame, the story text is moved to the next linked frame.

To delete a linked frame:

1. Click the border of the rightmost text frame to select it (the border turns solid) and press **Delete**.

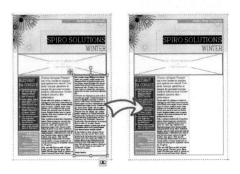

2. Select the centre frame again.

The centre frame now shows two different buttons, ⊞ **AutoFlow** and ▣ **Overflow**.

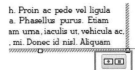

These show that the frame contains more story text that can actually be displayed. We'll tell you more about the function of the frame buttons later.

Working with text frames

Frames can have multiple columns. This can help simplify the layout design as it takes the worry out of aligning multiple frames. Let's look at this now.

To change the frame layout:

1. With the frame selected, click and drag the centre right resize handle to the right-hand margin. The text expands to fill the frame.

2. On the Text context toolbar, set the column number to **2**.

The text frame updates to contain 2 columns. Notice that the text also now fits in the frame and that there is no longer any overflow, as indicated by the ▣ button.

🏹 To access advanced frame properties, click 🖼 **Frame Setup.** In the dialog you can set other properties such as gutter and padding options.

Next we'll add a familiar 'drop caps' format to the first paragraph.

To add drop caps formatting to text:

1. Double-click to select the first word in the first paragraph of the text frame.

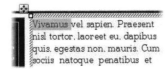

2. In the **Format** menu, click **Drop Cap...**

3. In the **Text Style** dialog:

- Set the **Drop cap type:** to **Dropped**.

- Click **OK** to accept the default settings.

  The drop cap style is applied to the first paragraph.

  Vivamus vel sapien.
  Praesent nisl tortor,
  laoreet eu, dapibus quis,
  egestas non, mauris. Cum sociis

To select, copy and paste text:

1. Triple-click on the longest paragraph in the text frame. The entire paragraph is selected.

2. On the Standard toolbar, click **Copy** (or press **Ctrl + C**).

3. Click anywhere in the text frame to create an insertion point. (As we are working with placeholder text you don't have to be accurate.)

4. Click **Paste** (or press **Ctrl + V**). The text is inserted.

The frame button has changed to indicate that we now have more story text than the text frame can hold. Let's fix this by linking the frame.

5. On the **Pages** tab, double-click page 2 to display it in the workspace.

6. Click in the centre frame to create an insertion point and then either quadruple-click or press **Ctrl + A** to select all of the text.

7. Press **Delete**.

You should now have an empty text frame.

8. Return to page 1 and select the main text frame.

9. Click the  **Overflow** button.

The cursor appears.

10. Return to page 2 and click once in the empty frame.

The hidden overflow text from the previous frame on page 1 appears as the two frames are now linked.

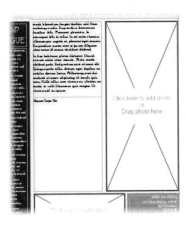

 Linking frames
You can create new linked frames (and link existing frames) in several ways.
See the topic *Linking text frames* in PagePlus Help for further details.

Getting creative with frames

For our final example, we're going to get a little more creative. Click on page 3 in the **Pages** tab and let's begin!

Before we dive in and start changing the design elements, we'll introduce one of the most useful tools in desktop publishing, the **layout grid**.

A layout grid is a set of non-printing guides that can help you to consistently place and align images. Using the grid can really enhance your layouts. Here, we'll show you how to create a 5 x 5 grid, however, if you want to know more, see the tutorials, *Page Layout Design* and *Creating Page Layouts*.

To create a layout grid:

1. On the Pages context toolbar, click  **Layout Guides**.

2. In the dialog:

- Set the **Rows** to **5**.

- Set the **Columns** to **5**.

- Click **OK**.

  The grid appears on the page.

The first thing that you'll notice is that the current layout of the objects does not match the new grid layout. We'll use some of the techniques used earlier and some new techniques to change this.

To delete multiple unwanted frames:

1. Click on the workspace just above the purple pull quote. Click and drag a section marquee around the pull quote objects and the centre text frame.

2. Press **Delete**.

You are left with the frame on the left of the page and the objects at the bottom.

To change the frame layout:

1. Click to select the left-most frame, drag the centre-right resize handle to expand the frame over four layout columns.

The text expands to fill the frame.

2. On the Text context toolbar, set the column number to **2**.

The text frame updates to contain 2 columns.

The pull quotes in this theme layout have been created by placing text frames on top of filled QuickShapes. However, an alternative method is to create a colour-filled text frame.

To create a colour-filled text frame:

1. On the Tools toolbar, click  **Standard Text Frame**.

2. On the page, align the mouse pointer with the edge of the rightmost layout column. Click and drag on the page to create a text frame that fits inside the layout column and is approximately 15.5 cm high.

3. Select the border of the frame (it will change to a solid outline) and on the **Swatches** tab, click the ▨ **Fill** button and then click the **Scheme Colour 3** swatch.

The fill is applied.

To create placeholder text:

1. Click inside the text frame to create an insertion point, and then type the word 'TIPS'. Press **Enter** to drop to the next line.

2. On the **Insert** menu, click **Fill with Placeholder Text** (or press **F5**).

3. Triple-click to select the longest paragraph and press **Delete**.

4. Next, click to place an insertion point at the end of each placeholder sentence and press **Enter**.

This will become our placeholder bullet text. Notice that it is tight against the frame edge? Although this is what we want normally, as this is a coloured frame, it would look better if we added some internal padding to the frame edge.

To add frame padding:

1. On the Text context toolbar, click **Frame Setup**.

2. In the dialog:

- On column 1, set the **Top** and **Bottom** to **0.2 cm**.

- Set the **Left Margin** to **0.2 cm**.

- Set the **Right Margin** to **0.2 cm**.

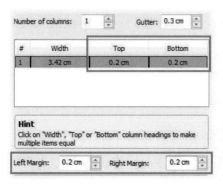

- Click **OK**.

  The frame is updated.

  Don't worry if you still can't see the text very well at the moment, we'll fix this in the next step.

Text styles

If you use styles to format text, you have the advantage that if you want to change the style, all instances of that formatting also update. Let's try this now.

To format text using text styles:

1. Press **Ctrl +A** to select all of the text in the frame.

2. On the Text context toolbar, in the styles drop-down list, select **Bullet List**.

   The style is applied to the text.

3. Next, double-click the word 'TIPS'.

4. On the Text context toolbar, in the styles drop-down list, select **Bullet List Heading**.

   The style is applied.

To update a text style:

1.   With the word 'TIPS' still selected, on the **Swatches** tab, click the  **Fill** button and then click the **Scheme Colour 1** swatch.

A fill is placed behind the text.

2.   Right-click the selected text and in the **Text Format** menu, click **Update Text Style**.

3.   In the warning dialog, click **Yes** to confirm the update to the style in the entire document.

4.   Finally, navigate to the other pages in the document. Notice that all of the bullet headings have been updated to match.

To finish this tutorial, we'll illustrate why we used scheme colours to colour our text and text frames.

When you switch to a different scheme, any elements (including text) in the publication that have been assigned one of the scheme colour numbers are updated with the corresponding colour from the new scheme. This means that we can give our newsletter a completely new look without any hard work!

To change the colour scheme:

- On the **Schemes** tab (at the bottom-right of the workspace), click to select a different scheme. (We chose **Abstract**.)

All of the schemed objects within the document update with the new scheme!

 To find out more, and for help creating your own schemes, see the *Colour Schemes* tutorial on p. 143.

You now know how to edit and format text, create new frame text objects, and edit text frame properties.

The skills you have acquired should be sufficient for most of your PagePlus projects, but you'll find more detailed information in PagePlus Help. If you haven't done so already, why not try the *Artistic Text* tutorial?

Artistic Text

In this tutorial, we'll show you how to create and manipulate artistic text. Artistic text is standalone text that can be typed directly onto a page. Its unique properties make it especially useful for titles, pull quotes, and other special-purpose text.

By the end of this tutorial you will be able to:

- Work with artistic text.

- Create, edit, and format text.

- Apply shadows, reflections, and other text effects.

- Create shaped text (or text-on-a-path).

Over the next few pages, we'll create a poster using artistic text objects. Along the way, you'll learn how to apply some of the stunning visual effects available in PagePlus.

Go to **http://go.serif.com/resources/PPX5** to download the following tutorial project file(s):

artistic.ppp

Let's begin...

- On the Standard toolbar, click 📂 **Open**.

- Locate the **artistic.ppp** file and click **Open**.

  The project opens in the workspace.

Although we are working with artistic text in this tutorial, many of the methods described below are applicable to both artistic and frame text. The special properties of artistic text allow you to:

- Stretch or squash the text to create a stylistic effect.

- Create shaped text by putting the text on a path.

Now let's create a new artistic text object...

To create artistic text:

1. On the Tools toolbar, on the Text flyout, click the Λ **Artistic Text Tool**.

2. Click anywhere on your page to set a text insertion point.

3. On the Text context toolbar, in the Text Styles drop-down list, select **TITLE**.

4. Type 'EXTREME GEAR'.

Now that our basic title is placed, let's make it a little more interesting.

To accurately resize and rotate artistic text:

1. With the text object still selected, on the **Transform** tab, ensure that the ⚙ **Lock Aspect Ratio** is off. (If not, click the button once.)

2. Change the Width to **28.0 cm** and then change the Height to **13.0 cm**.

3. Finally, rotate the object by **5°**. (For quick rotation, use the rotation 'lollipop' handle.)

4. Click and drag the ⊞ **Move** button located just above the upper-left corner of the object (or click and drag on the object's border) to drag the object into position as illustrated.

The title already has a lot more impact, but we can make it even more powerful by applying a gradient fill.

To apply a gradient fill:

1. Click the border of the text object to select it (the border turns solid) and then click on the **Swatches** tab.

2. Expand the ◢ ˙ **Gradient Fills** flyout and select **Linear**.

3. Click the **Linear Fill 14** swatch to apply it to the text.

The gradient colour spread works well, but we can make it fit the overall colour scheme better by changing it to use scheme colours.

4.

To edit a gradient fill:

1. Ensure the text object is selected and then on the Tools toolbar, click the 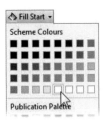 **Fill Tool**.

The object's fill path is displayed.

2. On the Fill context toolbar:

- In the **Fill Start** drop-down list, select swatch 5 on the Scheme 5 row.

- In the **Fill End** drop-down list, select swatch 5 on the Scheme 4 row.

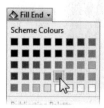

3. (Optional) You can also adjust the fill path by clicking and dragging the fill path nodes.

The title is almost complete; however, let's make it look really special by adding a reflection effect.

To apply a reflection effect:

1. With the text object selected, go to the **Styles** tab and in the categories drop-down list, select **Reflection**.

2. In the **Artistic Text Reflections** sub-category (you may need to scroll down), click the **Text Reflection 03 : FilterEffects** preset.

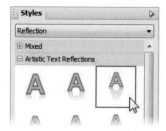

The reflection is applied.

To edit a reflection effect:

1. With the text object selected, on the Attributes toolbar, click the *fx* **Filter Effects** button.

2. Drag the dialog to the side so that you can see the text on the page. In the dialog:

   - Drag the **Offset** slider to the left until the reflection sits just below the text.

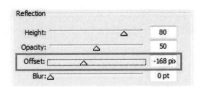

   - Click **OK**.

The reflection is updated.

For the final step, we are going to add the company website URL to the poster. For that extra special touch, we'll create it on a curved path.

To place text on a path:

1. On the Tools toolbar, on the Text flyout, click the **A** **Artistic Text Tool**.

2. Click anywhere on your page to create a text insertion point and on the Text context toolbar, set the font size to **48 pt**.

3. Go to the **Swatches** tab, click the **A** **Text** button and then click the **Scheme Colour 4** swatch. Set the **Tint** to **-50%**.

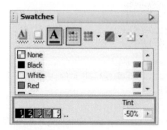

4. On the **Insert** menu, select **Information > User Details...**

5. In the dialog, select **Work Web** and click **OK**.

The company URL stored in the **User Details** is inserted on the page. (**Note:** We updated our User Details to match this scenario.)

6. On the Text context toolbar, in the **Path Text** drop-down list, select **Path - Wave**. The path is applied.

7. To stretch the path, drag the Start and End nodes (yellow highlight).

8. To adjust the slope of the path, click on a Start or End node and then drag its curve handle (blue highlight).

9. (Optional) Resize the text object by clicking and dragging the top and side edge resize handles.

10. Finally, click and drag the ⊞ **Move** button, or the object border, to move the object into position just below and to the left of the two images.

The poster is complete!

However, we'll take this opportunity to illustrate why we used scheme colours to colour our text...

To change the colour scheme:

- On the **Schemes** tab, click to select a different scheme. (The **Schemes** tab is collapsed by default at the bottom right of the studio.) We selected **Scheme 3**.

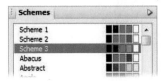

All of the schemed objects update!

This makes it easy to change the overall look and feel of your publication without any extra work. To find out more, and for help creating your own schemes, see the *Colour Schemes* tutorial on p. 143.

We hope that you've enjoyed this tutorial. You should now be quite adept at using artistic text. If you haven't done so already, why not try the *Frame Text* tutorial on p. 19? Have fun!

Pictures

The right pictures can make your publication stand out from the crowd. PagePlus offers a variety of tools and techniques for working with the pictures within your publication. In this tutorial, we'll start with a theme layout, then we'll show you how to add your own pictures, crop them, apply some basic image adjustments, and wrap text around the picture.

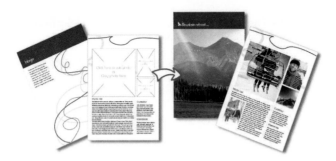

By the end of this tutorial you will be able to:

- Add and replace pictures.

- Use the **Media Bar**.

- Pan, zoom, and crop pictures.

- Apply image adjustments.

- Apply wrap to an image.

- Insert an inline image.

Let's begin...

1. On the **File** menu, click **New > New from Startup Wizard**.

2. In the **Create** section, click **Use Design Template**.

3. In the dialog:

- In the **Theme Layouts** list on the left, expand the **Illustrative** category and select the **Tickle** sub-category.

- In the centre pane, select the **Brochure** template.

- In the Scheme drop-down list, select **Scheme 2**.

- In the right **Pages** pane, select pages 1 and **3**.

- Click **OK**.

4. In the **User Details** dialog, make any necessary changes and click **Update**.

The layout opens in the workspace.

Before we do anything else, we'll customize the title.

5.   Click and drag on the word 'Integer' to select it.

6.   Type 'Mountain retreat...'

Our title is complete! Let's move on and start adding some pictures.

On the **Pages** tab, double-click the page 2 thumbnail to display the page in the workspace.

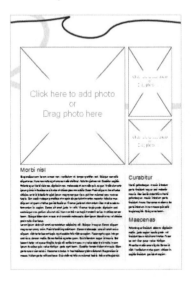

Adding pictures

This theme layout page provides three 'placeholder' picture frames for you to add your own photos.

You can add pictures individually by clicking directly on a placeholder, or you can add multiple pictures to the **Media Bar** and then drag them onto the frames as you need them. We'll demonstrate both methods. We'll be using the sample images installed with PagePlus. However, you can use your own images if you prefer.

To add a single picture to a frame :

1. Click inside the large picture frame. The **Import Picture** dialog opens.

2. In the **Import Picture** dialog, browse to your **Images** folder.

> 📌 In a standard installation, the Images folder is found in
> **C:\Program Files\Serif\PagePlus\X5\Images**
> However, the path may differ if you are running a 64 bit operating system or if you changed the installation location.

3. Select the ski-lift picture (5261963.jpg) and click **Open**.

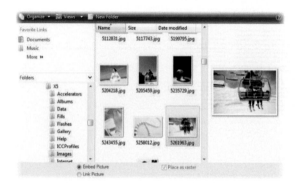

The picture is added to the frame and scaled to fit.

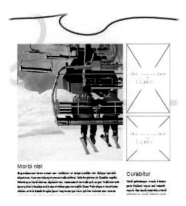

When the picture is selected, note that the picture frame toolbar displays in the lower-right corner.

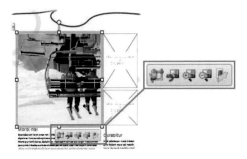

You can use these tools to adjust your picture inside the frame.

To adjust a picture inside a frame:

- To reposition the picture inside the frame, click 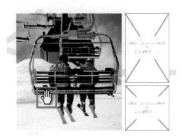 **Pan**, and then click and drag on the picture with the 🖑 cursor.

- To rotate the picture anti-clockwise, in 90° increments, click 🖼 **Rotate**.

- To zoom in or out of the picture, click 🖼 **Zoom In** or 🖼 **Zoom Out**.

- To replace the picture, click 🖼 **Replace Picture**, browse to and select a new picture, then click **Open**.

Using the Media Bar

If you're working with lots of pictures, or are not sure which of your pictures will work best in your publication, you might prefer to add them to the **Media Bar** before adding them to the layout. You can also use the albums included with PagePlus.

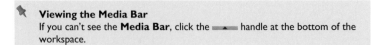

Viewing the Media Bar
If you can't see the **Media Bar**, click the ▬▬ handle at the bottom of the workspace.

To add images to the Media Bar:

1. By default, the **Media Bar**, displays a **Temporary Album**. If not, select this in the rightmost drop-down list.

2. Click in the blank area of the tab.

- or -

Click  **Add Image**.

In the **Import Picture** dialog, navigate to the folder where you keep your images.

3. Select your files and click **Open**. The photos are displayed as thumbnails on the **Media Bar**.

You can always save your temporary album to use in other publications. Click **Add To** and then click **New Album**.

To use images in the Media Bar:

1. On the **Media Bar**, in the rightmost drop-down list, select the **PagePlus X5 Tutorial Images** album.

2. Drag the photo of the couple outside the cabin (3176257.jpg) onto the upper-right picture frame.

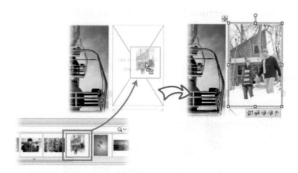

3. Drag the photo of the mountain (4568191.jpg) from the **Media Bar** onto the lower-left frame.

Once you've added pictures to frames, it's easy to replace them.

Let's change the top-right photo...

To replace a picture:

* Drag the photo of the man holding skis (30380107.jpg) from the **Media Bar** onto the upper-right frame.

  - or —

* Click the **Replace Picture** button and browse to the new image.

The page is looking pretty good. Let's now have a look at page 1. Along the way, we'll show you some more image techniques. First of all, on the **Pages** tab, double-click the page 1 thumbnail.

We're going to add an image to fill this page, but first of all we need to delete the elements that will obstruct our image.

To delete unwanted objects:

1.   (Optional) On the **View** toolbar, click **Full Page**.

2.   Position the pointer on the workspace in line with the 'Mountain retreat' text box.

3.   Click and drag a selection marquee over all of the elements on the white section of the page.

4.   Press the **Delete** key.

Now that we've created the space, let's add an image.

To insert a picture frame:

1. On the Tools toolbar, on the Picture flyout, click the ⊠
Rectangular Picture Frame.

2. Position the cursor at the left edge of the page, just below the green
banner. Click and drag to create a frame that fills the 'white' area of
the page.

3. Drag the photo of the mountain and rainbow (5117743.jpg) from the
Media Bar onto the picture frame.

4. Click the 🖾 **Zoom In** button a couple of time to zoom into the
image, then click the 🖾 **Pan** button to position the image so that the
rainbow starts in the corner.

Applying image adjustments

When you select a picture, the Picture context toolbar displays at the top of the workspace, automatically.

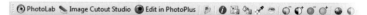

This toolbar provides quick and easy access to key picture-related controls—replace, resize, recolour, and so on—and also lets you apply useful image adjustments, such as red eye removal and brightness and contrast adjustments, with a single click.

We can improve our cover photo by applying a contrast adjustment.

To apply an image adjustment:

- With the picture frame selected, on the Picture context toolbar, click
   Increase Contrast. Repeat as required.

- (Optional) Experiment with the other adjustments provided on the
  Picture context toolbar to see how they affect the photos on your
  poster.

Advanced image adjustments

PagePlus includes a powerful mix of advanced image correction and adjustment
tools— including **levels**, **colour balance**, **channel mixer**, **HSL**, and
Unsharp Mask—and a selection of creative effects such as **Diffuse Glow**
and **Gaussian Blur**. The adjustments and effects are applied from the
PhotoLab dialog, which you can open by clicking ⊙ **PhotoLab** on the
Picture context toolbar.

For more information, see PagePlus Help.

Advanced image adjustments (continued)

Creating anchored objects

If you are working with text and images in a publication, you can obtain fine control over object positioning using object anchoring. We'll introduce this by adding a small inline image to the cover title.

To add an inline image:

1. Click on the **Gallery** tab and select the **Silhouettes** category.

2. In the **Birds** sub-category, drag **Bird3** onto the page.

3. Resize the silhouette so that it fits the size of the text. If you haven't done so already, drag it into position next to the title.

4. Click on the **Swatches** tab, and change the **Fill** colour to **Scheme Colour 3**.

5. On the **Arrange** menu, click **Anchor Object...**

6. In the **Anchored Objects Properties** dialog:

- Select **Position inline as character**.

- In the **Align with text** drop-down list, select **Middle**.

- Click **OK**.

The image is anchored to the text as an inline character.

 Anchored objects
When you anchor an object to a body of text, it remains with text at all times.

There are two ways to anchor objects in PagePlus:
• Float with text.
• Position inline as character.

For detailed information, see *Anchoring objects* in PagePlus Help.

That completes the front cover.

Applying wrap settings

To finish the tutorial we'll look at wrapping text around an image. Let's add another image to page 2.

To apply wrap settings:

1. On the **Pages** tab, double-click the page 2 thumbnail.

2. Drag the photo of the couple outside the cabin (3176257.jpg) from the **Media Bar** onto the page.

3. Resize the image so that it's approximately 5.5cm wide and fits just below the second line of text in the text frame.

4.   With the image selected, click ▣ **Wrap Settings** on the **Arrange** toolbar.

5.   In the **Wrapping** dialog:

- In the **Wrapping** section, select **Tight**.

- In the **Wrap To** section, select **Largest Side**.

- In the **Distance from text** section, enter **0.3 cm** in all four of the value boxes.

- Click **OK**.

The text wraps around the image. As this picture looks a bit too big, we'll finish by applying a crop.

To crop a picture:

1. Select the photo we've just added, then on the Crop flyout, click the ⛝ **Square Crop Tool**.

2. Click and drag the left edge handle inwards, as illustrated, and the top handle downwards, so that there are three lines of text above the image.

3. (Optional) To reposition a cropped image inside its frame, click and drag on the image (the cursor temporarily changes to **Pan**).

That's it! We've reached the end of this tutorial on pictures. We hope that you have enjoyed working through these simple exercises. You should be much more familiar with the techniques we've explored and able to confidently add pictures to your own publications.

Styles & Objects

PagePlus offers a variety of Gallery objects and styles to help you to easily enhance your text and images. Turn a simple holiday snap into a work of art with these simple steps.

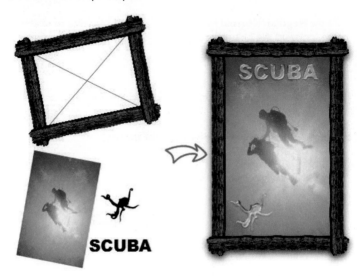

In this tutorial, we will:

- Add a Gallery picture frame to an image.

- Add a drop shadow effect.

- Add a Gallery object to a page.

- Apply pre-defined styles to objects and text.

Let's begin...

1. On the **File** menu, click **New > New from Startup Wizard**.

2. In the **Create** section, click **Start New Publication**.

3. In the **Regular/Normal** category, in the large pane, click to select the (portrait) **A4** or **Letter** thumbnail.

4. Click **OK**.

   A new blank document opens in the workspace.

To add a Gallery picture frame to an image:

1. On the **Gallery** tab, in the **Picture Frames** category, click and drag any frame thumbnail onto the page.

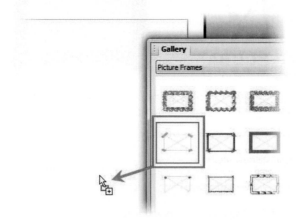

2.   With the frame selected, click and drag the square handles to resize it to fit the page.

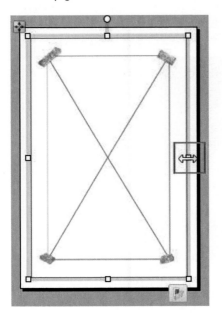

3.   On the **Media Bar**, in the rightmost drop-down list, select the **PagePlus X5 Tutorial Images** album.

   Viewing the Media Bar
If you can't see the **Media Bar**, click the ▂▂▄▄ handle at the bottom of the workspace.

4. Drag the photo of the scuba divers (34592157.jpg) onto the frame. The image is added to the frame.

To edit the position of the image inside the frame, use the tools on the picture frame toolbar located beneath the frame. For more information, see the *Pictures* tutorial on p. 53.

5.   To change the frame, simply drag a different thumbnail onto the image from the Gallery.

To add a drop shadow:

1.   With your image selected, click on the **Styles** tab.

2.   In the category drop-down list, select **Shadows**.

3. In the **Drop Shadow** sub-category, click on a style thumbnail to apply it.

Let's now add some artistic text to our photo. We'll then apply one of the styles in the **Styles** tab.

To apply style formatting to text:

1. On the Tools toolbar, click the A **Artistic Text Tool**.

2. Click somewhere on your image to create an insertion point.

3. On the Text context toolbar, set the font to **Arial Black** and the size to **72 pt**.

4. Type a title for your image.

5. Click the text object's border to select it.

6. On the **Styles** tab, select the **Presets - Materials** category from the drop-down list.

7. In the **Glass** sub-category, click the **Glass 01** thumbnail.

The effect is applied to the text.

To apply style formatting to a Gallery object:

1. Click on the **Gallery** tab and select the **Silhouettes** category.

2. Choose a silhouette from one of the sub-categories (we chose **Octopus** form the **Creatures** sub-category) and then drag the silhouette to the page.

3. Resize and reposition the object as necessary.

4. On the **Styles** tab, select the **Presets - Materials** category from the drop-down list.

5. In the **Glass** sub-category, click the **Glass 01** thumbnail. The object updates to match the style of the text.

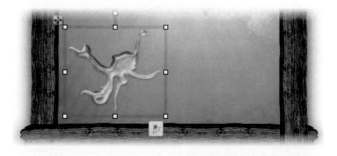

Why not experiment with some of the other styles to create some really interesting textures and effects?

That's it! Using the **Gallery** and **Styles** tabs we've created a stunning holiday snapshot. Why not apply some of these techniques to your own images? Have fun!

Master Pages

Some elements of your design will appear on every page of your publication. By using master pages, you can achieve consistency throughout your publication, and save yourself a lot of time and effort in the process!

By the end of this tutorial you will be able to:

- Add background images to a master page.

- Create a watermark.

- Apply a master page to a document.

- Work with multiple master pages.

Why use master pages?

Master pages are background pages, like sheets of extra paper behind your main publication pages. Every page can have one master page assigned to it and a given master page can be shared by any number of main pages.

Creating a consistent design is simple when you use a master page. When you add text frames, pictures, or other elements to the master page, they appear in the same position on all document pages that use that master page. Content placed on standard pages is displayed in front of the master page elements. This makes it easy to create a consistent design throughout your publication.

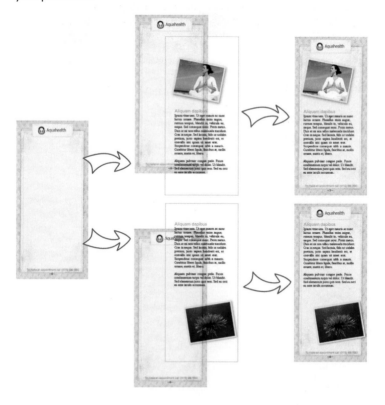

What you place on a master page is entirely up to you and often depends on the type of publication you are creating. Typical elements that you'd place on a master page include:

- background images (patterns, watermarks etc.).

- company name and/or logo.

- page number (using an automatic field).

- contact details.

Master pages simplify document maintenance as objects placed on a master page only need updating once. (If you didn't use a master page, you'd have to update the object on each individual page of the document.)

To demonstrate master pages, we've created a simple tri-fold flyer, **flyer.ppp**, which we have provided for you. In this tutorial, we'll enhance the layout by applying a background design with a master page.

Go to **http://go.serif.com/resources/PPX5** to download the following tutorial project file(s):

◎ **flyer.ppp**

Let's begin...

- On the Standard toolbar, click **Open**.

- Locate the **flyer.ppp** file and click **Open**.

  The project opens in the workspace. Before we start, take a moment to familiarize yourself with the document layout by double-clicking the pages in the **Pages** tab.

 Tri-fold flyer
We've already created placeholder content within this document. However, to create a tri-fold flyer from scratch:
- From the **Startup Wizard**, click **Start New Publication**.
- Click the **Folded** category and then click the **Other** sub-category.
- Click **Side Z-fold Menu**.
- Click **OK**.

To create a master page background:

1. On the **Pages** tab, expand the **Master Pages** pane. Notice that the document currently has a single, blank master page. Let's edit this now.

2. Double-click the 'MasterA' page thumbnail to display the page in the workspace.

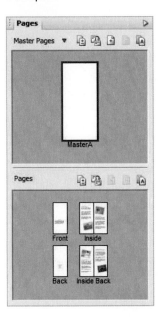

3. On the Tools toolbar, in the Picture flyout, click the ⊠ **Rectangular Picture Frame**.

4. Click and drag from the top left corner of the page to the bottom right to place the frame so that it covers the entire page.

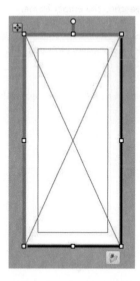

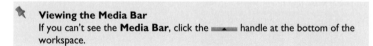

Viewing the Media Bar
If you can't see the **Media Bar**, click the ▬▲▬ handle at the bottom of the workspace.

5. On the **Media Bar**, in the rightmost drop-down list, select the **PagePlus X5 Tutorial Images** album.

6. Drag the **Leaf Background.jpg** image onto the empty frame.

The background is placed inside the frame.

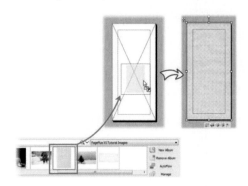

7. On the Tools toolbar, click the ⊠ **Rectangular Picture Frame**.

8. Click and drag on the page to place another frame, approximately 9 cm x 20.5 cm.

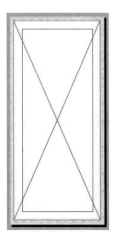

9. On the **Align** tab, select **Relative to: Page** and then, click  **Centre Vertically** and ⚏ **Centre Horizontally**.

10. Drag the **panel_quarter.png** image from the **Media Bar** and onto the frame.

By default, the image is cropped to best fit. However, this time, we'll need to make an adjustment.

> 🔖 We've taken some of the following screenshots with ☐ **Trimmed Page Mode** on for clarity. You'll find this button on the Hintline toolbar and the bottom of the workspace.

11. On the Picture context toolbar:

- Click  **Frame Properties**.

- In the dialog, click **Stretch to Fit** and click **OK**.

Your page should resemble ours.

12. Finally, we'll place a smaller panel to hold our logo. Click the ⊠ **Rectangular Picture Frame** and drag on the page to place a small, 6 cm x 2 cm frame at the top of the page.

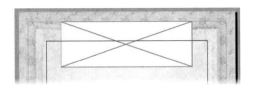

13. On the **Align** tab, select **Relative to: Page** and then, click ⬆ **Centre Horizontally**.

14. Drag the **panel_quarter.png** image from the **Media Bar** and onto the frame. Once again the image is cropped to best fit.

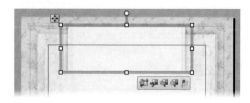

15. On the Picture context toolbar:

- Click **Frame Properties**.

- In the dialog, click **Stretch to Fit** and click **OK**.

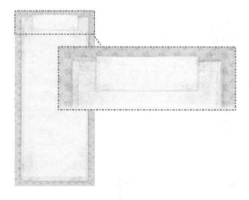

To add contact details:

1. On the Tools toolbar, click the ▣ **Standard Text Frame**.

2. Click and drag across the bottom of the page to place a frame approximately 8.5 cm wide and 0.5 cm high.

3. Go to the **Text Styles** tab (at the left of the workspace) and click the **Footer** paragraph style.

(If you can't see the **Footer** style, select the **Show All** option.)

4. In the text frame, type 'To make an appointment call', and then click **Insert > Information > User Details...**

5. In the dialog, select **Work Phone** from the list and click **OK**. The phone number is added to the text frame.

6. Finally, drag the text frame into position at the bottom of the page.

We extended our background image a little so that the text fits nicely just below the margin guide.

To return to normal view:

1. Double-click a normal page thumbnail on the **Pages** tab.

2. Click through pages on the **Pages** tab, or click the arrows on the Hintline toolbar, to view the pages.

The design suits the inner pages well, but it looks a little boring for the cover of the folded flyer. What we need is a different design for the front and back pages. We can easily do this by creating a second master page, and we can save time and effort by reusing some of the work that we've already done!

To create a second master page:

1. On the **Pages** tab, double-click the 'MasterA' page thumbnail to display the page in the workspace.

2. Click **Page Manager** and in the dialog:

- Select the **Add** tab.

- Select the **Copy layers from** option. The **Copy objects** option is selected by default.

- Click **OK**.

> The **Add** button on the **Pages** tab is a shortcut to adding a blank page to your document. This is ideal if you want to create an entirely different style of master page and don't need to reuse any objects.

The duplicate master page, **MasterB**, is displayed in the workspace and as a thumbnail in the **Pages** tab. (Click **Change Page Orientation** if necessary.)

If you have landscape and portrait pages in your document, you can change the orientation of a master page to match.
- On the **Pages** tab, select the appropriate master page thumbnail.
- Click 🖺 **Change Page Orientation**. The page updates.

Now we have our starting point, let's make some changes.

To delete multiple unwanted objects:

1. On the Tools toolbar, click the ▶ **Pointer Tool**.

2. Select the 'contact' text frame at the bottom of the page and press the **Delete** key.

To add a watermark:

1. On the Tools toolbar, in the Picture flyout, click the ⊠ **Rectangular Picture Frame**.

2. Click and drag on the page to place a frame within the page margin guides.

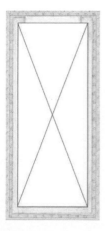

3. On the **Media Bar**, in the rightmost drop-down list, ensure the **PagePlus X5 Tutorial Images** album is displayed.

4. Drag the image of the meditating woman (5204218.jpg) onto the empty frame.

5. Click the 🔲 **Pan** button and pan the image further to the right.

6. On the **Transparency** tab, click the **Solid Transparency 70%** swatch.

The watermark is almost complete, but for a really professional look, we'll add a tint to match the colour scheme.

7. On the **Swatches** tab, click the **Fill** button and then click **Scheme Colour 4**.

8. To darken the colour, reduce the **Tint** value to **-50%**.

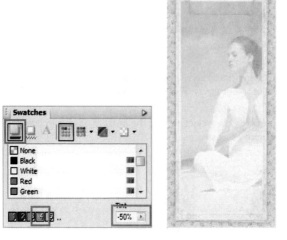

To complete the design, let's move the logo background banner to the bottom of the page.

To adjust the logo banner:

1. On the Tools toolbar, click the **Pointer Tool**.

2. Select the small rectangular banner and on the Arrange toolbar, click **Bring to Front**.

3. On the **Transform** tab, change the width to 9.5 cm. The height updates automatically as the aspect ratio is locked.

4. Finally, position the object so that the bottom edge is in line with the lower margin as illustrated.

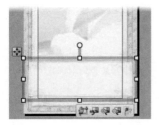

Now we've completed our second master page design, we need to assign it to the front and back pages of our flyer.

To assign a master page:

1. On the **Pages** tab, double-click on the 'Front' page thumbnail to return to normal view.

2. Drag and drop the **MasterB** thumbnail onto the **Front** page thumbnail.

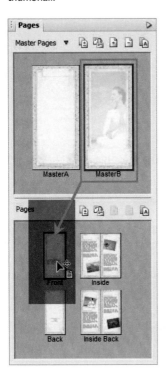

The master page is assigned.

3. Repeat step 2 and 3 to assign 'Master B' to the 'Back' page.

To check master page assignment:

- On the **Pages** tab, click 🔲 **Show Page Names**. The assigned master pages are displayed on each page thumbnail.

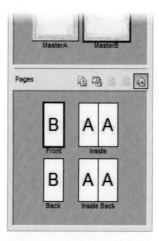

- Click the button again to return to the normal thumbnail view.

We added a modified logo from LogoStudio to the small panel at the top. For more information on how to do this, see either the **How To** tab, or the tutorial *LogoStudio* on p. 104.

That's it! You have successfully created and assigned multiple master pages to a publication. Why not explore this technique in your own documents? Have fun!

 In PagePlus X5, it's also possible to assign several master pages to a single page, creating a 'layered' effect. This can be useful when you want to use some elements, e.g., a background graphic or colour, on all pages, and other elements on only certain pages of the document. Assigning multiple master pages to a page is done from the **Layers** tab. For a detailed look at master pages and their advanced features, see PagePlus Help.

LogoStudio

LogoStudio makes it easy to create and edit logos in isolation from other page elements. You can create your own logos from scratch, or choose from a range of logo templates and samples. We'll introduce you to some of the powerful LogoStudio features in this tutorial.

By the end of this tutorial you will be able to:

- Insert a LogoStudio logo.

- Modify an existing logo.

- Convert an existing design to a LogoStudio logo.

- Create a logo from scratch.

- Add a logo design to the **Gallery** tab.

Let's begin...

1. On the **File** menu, click **New > New from Startup Wizard**.

2. In the **Create** section, click **Start New Publication**.

3. In the dialog, select a standard page size and click **OK**.

The page opens in the workspace.

Next, we'll have a look at adding our first logo to the page. It's time to enter **LogoStudio**!

 The first time you go into **LogoStudio**, take a moment to familiarize yourself with the layout of the tabs as they may be a little different form your normal studio layout.

To create a logo from an existing template:

1. On the Tools toolbar, click **Insert Logo**.

2. In the **Insert Logo** dialog, select a design template from the **Logos** pane, and then choose your template layout from the **Pages** pane. (These differ depending on the template chosen.)

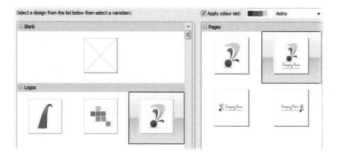

3. In the upper right corner of the dialog:

- To apply the colour scheme of the publication, clear the **Apply colour set** check box.

  - or -

- To apply a colour set (a specially designed logo scheme), select the **Apply colour set** check box, and then select a colour set from the drop-down list.

The logo preview updates to match your colour set selection.

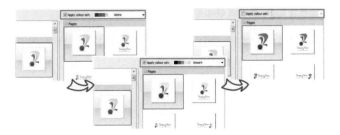

4. Click **Open**.

5. (Optional) If you have chosen a logo containing text objects, the **Customize Your Logo** dialog opens. Edit the Name and Motto as necessary and click **OK** to complete the design and exit.

6. To insert the logo at default size, click on your page; to set the size of the logo, click and drag out a region and release the mouse button.

To add a logo from the Gallery:

1. On the **Gallery** tab, select the **Logos** category from the drop-down menu.

2. Scroll to you chosen logo, then click and drag it from the tab onto the page.

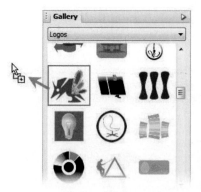

An **Insert Logo** dialog opens.

3.   In the dialog:

- To apply the colour scheme of the publication, clear the **Apply colour set** check box.

  - or -

- To apply a colour set (a specially designed logo scheme), select the **Apply colour set** check box, and then select a colour set from the drop-down list.

- In the **Designs** pane, choose your design.

- (Optional) In the **Name** text box, type your company name.

- Amend the **Motto** text.

- Click **OK**.

4.   The logo is placed on the page. Resize as necessary.

To edit an existing logo:

1. Click the  **Edit in LogoStudio** button that displays on the control bar under the selected logo.

2. LogoStudio opens with your object(s) zoomed in to fit your workspace.

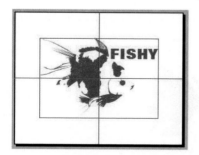

You'll find this logo example in the **Samples** section of the **Insert Logo** dialog.

3. To customize your logo design, use the interactive **How To** tab elements, or the traditional PagePlus creation tools.

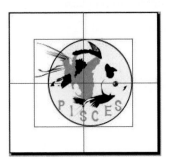

In this logo we edited the fish colour, text and added a **Quick Circle**.

4. Click **Close LogoStudio** to return to the main PagePlus workspace and view your logo on the page.

To convert an existing design to a logo:

1. Select the object(s) you want to convert to your logo.

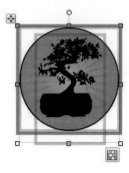

2. On the **Tools** menu, click **Convert To > Logo...**

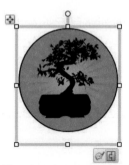

Your logo is converted and will now behave in the same way as other logos.

To create a logo from scratch:

1. On the Tools toolbar, click 🖉 **Insert Logo**.

2. In the **Insert Logo** dialog, select the blank thumbnail from the Blank section in the left pane.

3. Click **Open**.

4.   Click or click and drag to place the logo on the page.

The LogoStudio environment opens automatically.

5.   To create your design, you can use the interactive **How To** tab elements, or the traditional PagePlus creation tools.

6.   To return to your original document, click ✕ **Close LogoStudio**. Your design is displayed on the page.

To add a logo to the Gallery:

1. On the **Gallery** tab, in the category drop-down list, select **My Designs**.

2. Press and hold the **Ctrl** key and drag a copy of the logo onto the **Gallery** tab.

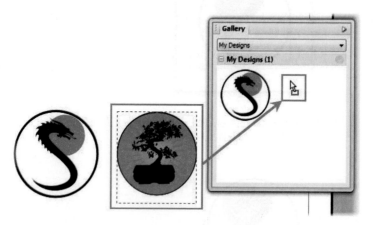

3. In the dialog, name your logo object and click **OK**.

A copy of the object appears in the tab and is now ready for use in all of your future projects!

💡 **Did you know that you can search the Gallery?**

- Click the **Tab Menu** button and then click **Find Design...**
- In the dialog, type all or part of the design name and click **Find Next**.

All designs containing the name will display in the tab. This is why it's so important to give you design a sensible name when you add it to the Gallery!

We hope that you've enjoyed this adventure into logo territory. Why not have a go at designing your own logos? Have fun!

Page Numbering

In this simple tutorial, we'll show you a useful way to combine master pages and page numbering. We'll also take a look at using mixed page number formats within a publication.

By the end of this tutorial you will be able to:

• Add page numbers to a master page.

• Promote an object from a master page.

• Create multiple sections using mixed number formats.

Let's begin...

1. On the **File** menu, click **New > New from Startup Wizard**.

2. In the **Create** section, click **Use Design Template**.

3. In the dialog:

- In the **Theme Layouts** list on the left, click the **Textured** category, then click **Vintage**.

- In the centre pane, select the **Brochure** template.

- In the **Pages** pane, select the first six pages.

- Click **OK**.

4. In the **User Details** dialog, make any necessary changes and click **Update**. The template opens as a new, six page document in the workspace. Each page is displayed in the **Pages** tab.

Now that we have a multi-page publication, let's add some page numbers! We can easily add page number to every page by simply adding them to the master page(s) of our publication. PagePlus does the rest!

 You can also add a page number to a header or footer by using the Header and Footer Wizard, found in **Insert > Headers and Footers...** Just follow the on-screen instructions. For more information, see PagePlus Help.

To add a page number to a master page:

1. On the **Pages** tab, expand the **Master Pages** pane and double-click the 'MasterA' page thumbnail to display the page.

2. Click the A **Artistic Text Tool**, and then click once just below the bottom margin. When you release the mouse button and can see a flashing text-insertion cursor, on the **Insert** menu, click **Information > Page Number**.

The automatic page number is inserted.

 At this stage, the number may display either as {n} or as an actual number and does not affect the following steps in any way. The number will update when viewed on a page (and not the master page).

3. Select the page number text:

- On the Text context toolbar, format your text as desired.

- On the Text context toolbar, click the ≣ **Align Centre** button.

- On the **Align** tab, ensure **Relative to: Page** is selected and then click ⚏ **Centre Horizontally**.

> 💡 Using centred alignment on your text means that as your page number extends from 1 to 2 to 3 characters, the entire number will remain centred.

4. On the **Pages** tab, click each of the page thumbnails to display them in the workspace.

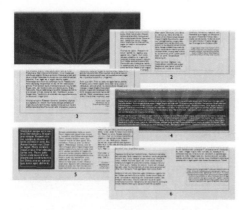

As you can see, the page number is displayed in the same place at the bottom of each page, with one exception, page 1. This is because there is a blue object that has been placed on that page. However, we can easily fix this by promoting the page number in this instance.

> ★ The next steps can be completed using any object placed on a master page.

To promote an object from a master page:

1. In the **Pages** tab, double-click the Page 1 thumbnail. The page is displayed in the workspace.

2. Starting with the Pointer on the workspace just off the page, click and drag to create a selection around the approximate position of the page number. If you don't succeed the first time, try a larger selection area.

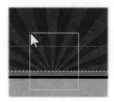

The page number object is selected.

3. Click **Promote from Master Page**.

4. With the object still selected, on the Arrange toolbar, click **Bring to Front**.

5. On the **Swatches** tab, ensure the **Text** button is selected and click a light coloured swatch. The text is updated and can be easily seen on the front page.

Special and mixed page number formats

In larger publications, it's common to see different styles of page numbers for different sections. For example, the contents pages may have roman numerals while the main body of the publication will have an arabic (standard) format. We'll briefly show you how to do this with the **Page Number Format** dialog.

To create publication page number sections:

1. On the **Format** menu, click **Page Number Format...**

2. On the lower left side of the dialog, beneath the **Section** pane, click **Add...**

3. In the **Add New Section** dialog, type the number "2" to start the new section at page 2 and click **OK**.

4. Repeat the step, this time starting the new section at page 4. Your dialog should resemble ours.

Pages	Format
1	1
2 - 3	2 - 3
4 - 6	4 - 6

Before we exit the dialog, we'll reformat our second section.

To format page numbers:

1. In **Section** pane, in the **Pages** column, click page 2-3.

2. In the **Style** pane, select **Lower Roman i, ii, iii, ...**

The format updates.

Pages	Format
1	1
2 - 3	ii - iii
4 - 6	4 - 6

3. In the **Numbering** section, clear the **Continue from previous section** option and type the number "1" (one) as your **First page number** (the format will update automatically when you click away from the input box).

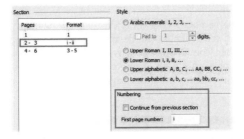

4. In **Section** pane, in the **Pages** column, click page 4-6, and in the **Numbering** section, clear the **Continue from previous section** option and type the number "1" (one) as your **First page number**. Leave the formatting set to **Arabic numerals 1, 2, 3, ...**

Once again, the section numbers are updated.

Pages	Format
1	1
2 - 3	i - ii
4 - 6	1 - 3

5. Click **OK** to exit the dialog.

On the **Pages** tab, you'll see that the numbering beneath the thumbnails has updated to show the new sections.

In a publication using the number styling we've created, it would be common practice not to see a number on the first page. In an earlier step, we promoted the number from the master page so that we could see it. In the same way, once an object has been promoted from a master page, we can also delete it without affecting the other pages.

To "delete" a promoted master page object:

1. Select the object to delete, in our case the page number. The **Revert to Master Page** button beneath the object shows that it is no longer associated to the master page.

2. Press the **Delete** key. The object is removed from the first page.

If you now view each page, you'll see how the numbers change in each section.

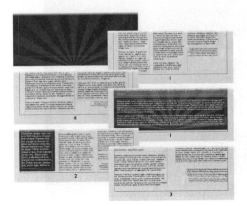

> When subsequent pages are added to your publication, they will use the number formatting assigned to the previous page.
>
> The recommended way to add new pages to a section is to display the last page of the section in the workspace, and then use the 🗋 **Page Manager** to add additional pages **after** your selected page. For more information, see PagePlus Help.

(Optional) Creating event tickets

Now that you know how to format page numbers, why not combine this with a 'small publication' document and automatically create sequentially numbered tickets? You could easily create individually numbered tickets for fund raisers, music gigs, club and sports events...

The possibilities are endless! Here is an example that is designed to be printed on standard business card paper to get you started.

> The entire ticket design is done on the master page of the **Wide Business Card** new publication type. When your design is complete, simply insert the number of pages that you wish to print so that the 'ticket' numbers increase automatically.

The ticket body:

- We used **Artistic text** for the main text (A) and formatted it appropriately with the **Swatches** tab and the Text context toolbar.

- To create visual interest, we used a **Gallery** object and applied a red fill (B).

- A text frame was used for the general ticket information (E) and formatted with the **Swatches** tab and the Text context toolbar.

- We placed a text frame object and inserted a page number (**Insert > Information > Page Number**) to create the ticket number (F). In the **Page Number Format** dialog, we set **Pad to 4 digits** (see note on next page).

You can prefix your automatic numbering with leading zeros using the **Page Number Format** option.

• In the **Page Number Forma** dialog, select the **Pad to** option and enter the number of digits you want the number to be. (For example, for numbers between 1 and 9999, pad to 4 digits.)

• Click **OK**. All page numbers below the set number of digits will be displayed with the correct number of leading zeros.

The ticket stub:

- We added a line and formatted it on the **Line** tab to create the stub separator.

- To create visual interest, we used a **Gallery** object and applied a red fill (D).

- To create the ticket stub number (C), we replicated the previous ticket number (F), and then rotated the frame by 90° and increased the size of the text.

- We replicated the main text objects (A) and rotated and reduced them to fit our stub (G).

Tables

Tables are a great way of displaying all forms of data quickly and easily.
They can also be used as layout tools. Price lists, menus, general lists,
school timetables, research data, opening times—all look best when
inserted into a table on your publication. The best part is that PagePlus
makes this easy to do.

In this tutorial, we'll show you how to:

- Import a table.

- Add and delete rows and columns.

- Apply **Auto Format**.

- Customize an existing **Auto Format**.

In this tutorial, we are going to add a price list to the back of a health spa flyer. To help you follow the tutorial, we've provided our file for you.

Go to **http://go.serif.com/resources/PPX5** to download the following tutorial project file(s):

flyer2.ppp

Let's begin...

- On the Standard toolbar, click **Open**.

- Browse to the **flyer2.ppp** file, click to select it and then click **Open**.

  The publication opens in the PagePlus workspace.

- On the **Pages** tab, double-click on the 'Back' page to display it.

We're ready to add our table.

To create a table:

1. On the Tools toolbar, click the ▦ **Table Tool**.

2. Position your mouse pointer over the left margin guide, just below the logo banner. Click and drag to create a table between the margin guides.

3. In the **Create Table** dialog:

- In the **Format** list, click **Dooly 3**.

- Set the **Number of rows** to **14**.

- Set the **Number of columns** to **2**.

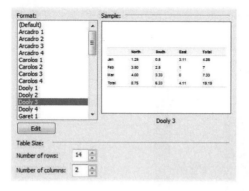

- Click **OK**.

  The two column table is added to our page.

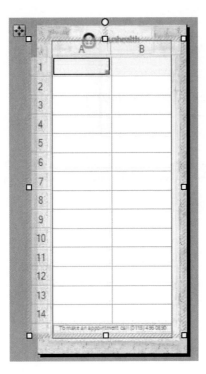

Let's now add the data to our table.

To add table data:

1. Click in the first cell of the table and type the word 'Treatment'.

2. Click in the next header cell and type 'Price'.

3. Press the right arrow. Notice that the cursor goes to the next available cell. Type 'Aromatherapy', and press the right arrow to move to the next cell.

4. Type '£65'.

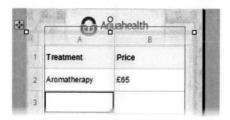

5. Complete the table using the treatments found in the flyer. (If you don't want to do this, simply add some text to the next 10 frames!)

Now that we've added all of the treatments, you'll notice that we have two rows left over. As they're not needed, we can delete them.

To delete a row:

1. Click inside the first cell that you want to delete and then drag over the other three empty cells.

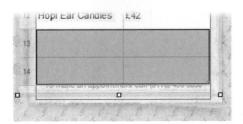

2. On the **Table** menu, click **Delete > Row(s)**.

3. The rows are deleted from the table.

We'll now show you how to add a column to your table.

To add a column:

1. With your table selected, click on the column header **B**. The whole column is highlighted.

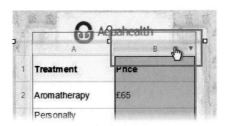

2. On the **Table** menu, click **Insert > Columns**.

3. In the dialog, select the **After selected cells** option and click **OK**.

A new column is added to the right of the table.

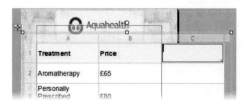

To resize a column:

1. With your table selected, click on the column header **B**.

2. Position the pointer on the divide between column headers **B** and **C**.

3. Drag to the left to reduce the width of column B so that the word 'Price' just fits.

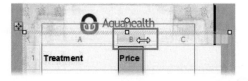

4. In the heading row of column C, type 'Duration'. Don't worry if the formatting is different, we'll fix this in a minute.

5. Click on column header **C** to select the column.

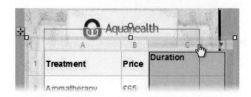

6. On the **Table** menu, click **Autofit to Contents > Column(s)**.

7. Finally, drag the right-centre handle of the table to the right so that it fits to the page margin again.

5	Thalasso Active	£20
6	Bright Eyes	£40
7	Intense Moisture Facial	£55

Now that the table fits nicely on the page, type the treatment duration information into the new column that you created.

Treatment	Price	Duration
Aromatherapy	£65	55 mins
Personally Prescribed Aromatherapy	£80	85 mins
Detoxifying Seaweed Wrap	£52	55 mins

You'll notice that the formatting is slightly different to that in the first two columns. We can fix this by re-applying the table **Auto Format**.

To apply table Auto Format:

1. Click on the table to select it.

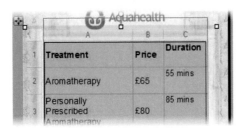

2. On the Table context toolbar, click 🔳 **Auto Format**.

3. In the **AutoFormat** dialog, in the **Format** pane, click **Dooly 3** and then click **OK**.

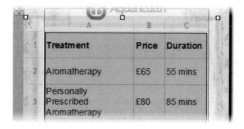

The table format is reapplied.

To create a custom table format:

1. On the **Table** menu, click **Edit AutoFormat...**

The **Table Formats** dialog opens, ready to edit the currently applied table format.

2. In the **Cell Style** pane, click **Odd Row** and then click **Edit...**

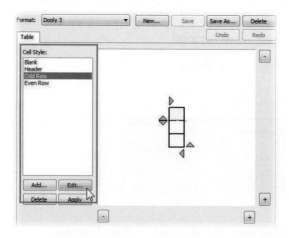

3. In the **Cell Properties** dialog:

- Click the **Font** tab.

- In the **Font** drop-down list, select **Life BT**.

- In the **Size** drop-down list, select **9 pt**.

- Click **OK**.

   The changes are displayed in the Preview pane.

4. In the **Cell Style** pane, click **Even Row** and then click **Edit...** and repeat step 3.

5. In the **Cell Style** pane, click **Header** and then click **Edit...**

6. In the **Cell Properties** dialog:

- Click the **Font** tab.

- In the **Font** drop-down list, select **Life BT**.

- Click **OK**.

7. Click **Save As...**

8. Type a name for your new format, for example 'Flyer', and click **OK**.

9. Finally, click **OK** to close the **Table Formats** dialog.

Your table is updated with the new format.

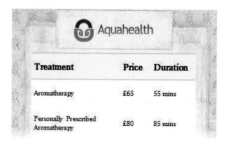

By formatting the table in this way, you will be able to quickly apply this style to any table in future publications with the 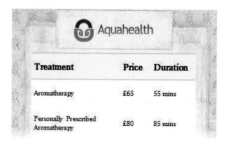 **Auto Format** button on the toolbar.

There are many more things that you can do with table formatting, for example, you can change cell colour to match your publication and create your own from scratch. You can also add inline images as in the product list example.

Why not create your own calendar with the 🗓 **Calendar Tool**? The formatting techniques are very similar and a Wizard will guide you through the initial setup.

Although beyond the scope of this tutorial, you'll find more information in the PagePlus Help and on the **How To** tab. Have fun!

Colour Schemes

When designing your publications, one of the most important factors to consider is colour. It sets the mood, sends a message and gets attention. But how do you select a colour palette that's right for your publication? In the first of the colour schemes tutorials, we'll introduce you to PagePlus colour schemes.

In the first section of this tutorial, we'll apply scheme colours to individual elements on a page. We'll then show you how you can edit and modify scheme colours.

By the end of this tutorial you will be able to:

- Apply a preset colour scheme from the **Scheme Manager**.

- Modify an existing colour scheme.

Let's begin...

1. On the **File** menu, click **New > New from Startup Wizard**.

2. In the **Create** section, click **Use Design Template**.

3. In the dialog:

- In the **Theme Layouts** list on the left, click the **Illustrative** category, then click **Spiro**.

- In the centre pane, select the **Small Address Label** template.

- Click **OK**.

    The page opens in the workspace.

The top half of our page contains a coloured banner. This is created using QuickShapes and text that have all been designed to use colour schemes. Let's look at this now by choosing a different scheme.

To apply a colour scheme:

1. At the bottom-right of the workspace, click **Schemes** to expand the **Schemes** tab.

You'll see an assortment of named schemes, each consisting of five basic colours. The colour scheme that is currently applied is highlighted.

2. On the **Schemes** tab, click to select **Scheme 2**.

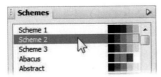

All schemed objects within the publication update with the new colours.

If you take a look at our design templates, you'll notice that these are also designed to use colour schemes so that you can change the look and feel quickly and easily.

Applying scheme colours to objects

The scheme colours work much like a paint-by-numbers system, where various regions and elements of a page layout are coded with numbers. In each scheme, a specific colour is assigned to each number. You can change or even apply a colour scheme at any point during the design process, but it's best practice to scheme your objects from the start. This gives you the most flexibility if you decide to change the look and feel of a publication.

 A publication can only have one colour scheme in use at any given time.

To apply a scheme colour to an object:

1. On the Tools toolbar, on the 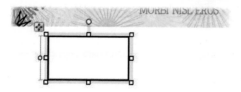 **QuickShape** flyout, click the **Quick Rectangle** and draw a large shape on the page.

2. Click to display the **Swatches** tab.

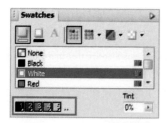

At the bottom of the tab, below the colour swatches, you'll see that the five main colours of the current colour scheme appear as numbered swatches.

3. Ensure that the shape is selected and on the **Swatches** tab:

- Click the **Fill** button and then click the scheme colour you want to apply to the shape's fill.

- Click the **Line** button and apply a different scheme colour to the shape's outline.

4. On the **Schemes** tab, click to apply a different colour scheme to the publication.

PagePlus applies the new scheme colours to the shape.

On the **Swatches** tab, notice that the colour scheme swatches have been replaced with the new scheme colours.

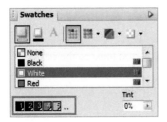

You can also apply scheme colours to text in the same way.

As you can see, when you create new elements in any publication, you can extend a colour scheme to your layout elements using the process just described.

If you copy an object that uses scheme colours to another PagePlus publication, the object will take on the colour scheme used in the new document.

You'll need to spend some time working out which colour combinations look best, but the mechanics of the process are simple.

Modifying colour schemes

If you've tried various colour schemes but haven't found one that's quite right for your document, you can modify any of the colours in an existing scheme to create a new one.

To modify a colour scheme:

1. On the **Swatches** tab click the ·· button (next to the colour swatches).

2. In the **Colour Scheme Designer** dialog, the current scheme colours are displayed.

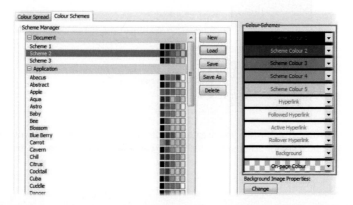

Each of the five scheme colours (plus **Hyperlink, Followed Hyperlink, Active Hyperlink** and **Rollover Hyperlink** colours) has its own drop-down list, showing available colours.

3. To set or change a scheme colour, simply click the button to expand the drop-down list, and then select a new colour.

4. **Optional step:** If the drop-down palette doesn't contain the colour you want to use, click **More Colours** to display the **Colour Selector**.

In the **Colour Selector** dialog, various controls allow you to choose a colour to apply or mix your own custom colours.

- The **Models** tab displays the colour space of the currently selected colour model.

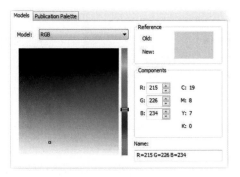

- The **Publication Palette** tab lets you modify the set of colours associated with the current publication.

- Click **OK** to save changes and exit the dialog.

5. When you have modified your scheme, click **OK** to apply it to your publication.

When you save your document, its current colour scheme is saved with the publication. However, if you want to use the scheme in other publications, you need to save it to the application. (To learn how to create and modify your colour schemes, see the tutorial, *Colour Schemes II* on p. 153.)

To save a scheme (application):

1. On the **Swatches** tab click the ⁚ button and ensure that the **Colour Schemes** tab is displayed.

2. In the **Colour Scheme** pane, the current document scheme colours are displayed.

3. To create a new scheme, click **Save As** and type in a new name and click **OK**.

- or -

To overwrite an existing scheme, click to select it and then, click **Save**.

4. The scheme library is updated to reflect the changes. If you have created a new scheme, it will appear at the bottom of the **Application** list.

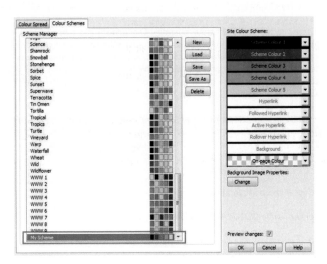

In future, you will be able to load your saved scheme from within any publication.

There are two types of colour scheme—**Document** and **Application**—that are saved in the library. An Application colour scheme is saved globally and can be loaded (applied) to any publication. A document colour scheme is template specific and is only available within a publication created from that template. However, you can save a copy of a Document (template) scheme as an application scheme if you want to use it in any other publication.

When a scheme is loaded, a copy of it is created as your publication scheme. You can modify this as much as you want and the changes will be saved with you publication. However, any changes you make will not update the Application scheme unless you explicitly choose to overwrite it.

To ensure that a publication is using the latest copy of an Application scheme, select it in the list and then click **Load**.

For more information, see PagePlus Help.

Colour Schemes II

There may be times when you want to create a new colour scheme from scratch, perhaps using colours from your company logo or an image that features in your PagePlus document or on your website. Creating a colour scheme that complements your images is also a good design technique.

By the end of this tutorial you will be able to:

• Create your own colour scheme from scratch using an image for colour reference.

Let's begin...

1.   On the **File** menu, click **New > New from Startup Wizard**.

2.   In the **Create** section, click **Start New Publication**.

3.   In the dialog, select a standard landscape page size and click **OK**.

   The page opens in the workspace.

Creating custom colour schemes from scratch

In PagePlus, there are two ways of creating a colour scheme, automatically starting with a base colour, or by choosing your colours from an image.

> ✎ You can use our sample photograph or any image of your choice. You'll find the sample photograph (34592157.jpg) in the **PagePlus X5 Tutorial Images** album in the **Media Bar**. (For more about using the **Media Bar**, see the *Quick Start* (p. 5) or *Pictures* (p. 53) tutorials.)

Creating a colour scheme from an image

One of the best ways of designing a colour scheme for your publication is to base it around the images that you've used. This way, it will tie all of the design elements together. We'll show you how to do this now.

To create colour scheme placeholders:

1.   Add your image to the page and resize it so that there is some white space around it.

2.   On the Tools toolbar, on the QuickShapes flyout, click the ▢ **Quick Rectangle**.

3. Draw a small square on the page next to the image.

4. With the shape still selected, on the **Edit** menu, click **Replicate...**

5. In the **Replicate** dialog:

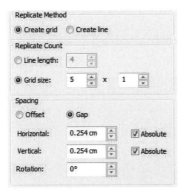

- In the **Replicate Method** section, click **Create grid**.

- In the **Replicate Count** section, set the **Grid size** to **5** wide by **1** high.

- Set the **Spacing** to **Gap** (we used the default setting of 0.254cm) and ensure that the **Absolute** checkbox is selected.

  The preview updates.

- Click **OK**.

  The squares have been replicated and aligned next to the image.

Next, we need to prepare our image and start choosing the colours for our scheme. First, we'll apply a filter to reduce the available colours, and then we'll use the colour picker to select individual colours.

To select colours from an image:

1. Select the image and then on the Picture context toolbar, click
PhotoLab.

2. In **PhotoLab**, click the **Effects** tab and then expand the **Style**
category. Click the **Pixelate** thumbnail.

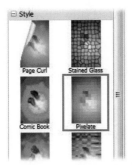

In the lower right **Trial Zone**, the **Pixelate** control displays.

3. Drag the **Cell Size** slider, to the left so that colours making up the
image blend into colour 'blocks,' as illustrated. You don't want the
blocks either too large or too small. We found **18 pix** worked well.
Click **Commit** when you are happy with the result.

4. To close **PhotoLab** and return to the PagePlus workspace, click **OK**.

5. Back on the page, select the first square you created, click the **Colour** tab, and then click the ✎ **Colour Picker**.

6. On the image, click and drag to select the first colour you want to add to your new colour scheme. Ideally, start with the darkest colour.

The popup colour sample updates as you drag to different areas of the image. When you are happy with the colour displayed in the sample, release the mouse button.

The selected colour is applied to the square, and added to the
Publication Palette on the **Swatches** tab.

7. Selecting each of the remaining squares in turn, repeat the previous
step to fill the shapes with four additional colours from your image.

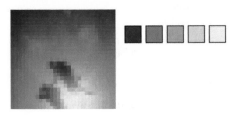

8. On the **Swatches** tab, scroll to the end of the palette swatches to
find your new custom colours displayed.

We're now ready to create our new colour scheme.

To create a scheme from selected colours:

1. On the **Swatches** tab, click ·· to open the **Colour Scheme Designer**.

2. Click the **Colour Spread** tab, then, in the Colour Scheme pane:

- Click the arrow next to **Scheme Colour 1** to expand the drop-down palette.

- Locate the colours you added in the previous steps.

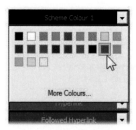

- Click the colour you want to assign to **Scheme Colour 1**.

The colour is applied.

3. Repeat step 2 to assign the remaining scheme colours.

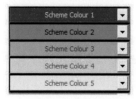

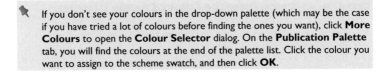

If you don't see your colours in the drop-down palette (which may be the case if you have tried a lot of colours before finding the ones you want), click **More Colours** to open the **Colour Selector** dialog. On the **Publication Palette** tab, you will find the colours at the end of the palette list. Click the colour you want to assign to the scheme swatch, and then click **OK**.

4. Click the **Colour Schemes** tab and then click **Save As**. Name your scheme in the dialog and click **OK**.

5. If you are happy with your colour scheme, click **OK** to exit the **Colour Scheme Designer**.

6. Click the **Swatches** tab. Note that the swatches at the bottom of the tab now display your custom scheme colours.

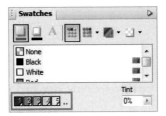

You can use these swatches to apply scheme colours to objects on your page.

If you have a basic colour in mind for your site, but you're not sure which colours to use with it, let the **Colour Scheme Designer** do most of the hard work! We're still going to start with a colour picked from the same image, but you can pick up your colour from anywhere!

Creating a scheme using the Colour Scheme Designer:

1. Add your image to the page and create a single QuickShape placeholder.

2. On the **Colour** tab, select **RGB** from the **Colour Mode** drop-down list.

Using the  **Colour Picker**, choose your base colour. This should be suitable for the 'middle' colour of the new scheme, not too light or too dark. (See the previous steps for how to do this.) Make a note of the R G B values.

3. On the **Tools** menu, click **Colour Scheme Designer...** (This way, you can still view the **Colour** tab for the colour reference.)

4. In the **Colour Scheme Designer** dialog, type in the RGB value from the colour tab into the respective input fields.

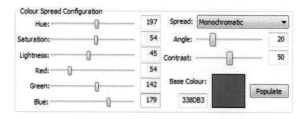

5. Select a spread type from the **Spread** drop-down list. These are based on standard Colour Theory principles. We selected **Monochromatic**.

6. (Optional) Increase the **Contrast** to increase the range in the colours. Change the **Angle** to alter where the colours are picked up from the colour wheel.

7. Click **Populate**.

- or -

For more control, click and drag the individual colour swatches onto a specific Scheme colour.

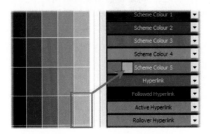

8. Click the **Colour Schemes** tab and then click **Save As**. Name your scheme in the dialog and click **OK**.

9. If you are happy with your colour scheme, click **OK** to exit the **Colour Scheme Designer**.

10. Click the **Swatches** tab. Note that the swatches at the bottom of the tab now display your custom scheme colours.

Congratulations, you've created a custom colour scheme from scratch! It's a relatively simple process, but one which we hope you'll find useful in your future PagePlus publications. For more information on the **Colour Scheme Designer**, see PagePlus Help. Have fun experimenting!

2 Theme Layouts

Theme Layouts

PagePlus provides a selection of **Theme Layout** templates that you can use as starting points for your own publications. We've even provided placeholders for your own images!

Theme Layouts templates are split into the following style categories-**Editorial**, **Graphical**, **Illustrative** and **Textured**. There are 40 different themes, each containing over 20 different document types which cover a wide range of layout styles. With this amount of choice, you're bound to find the right layout for your needs!

Each theme includes the following document types:

- Address Labels
- Brochures
- Business Cards
- Business Forms
- Compliment Slips
- Emails
- Envelopes
- Flyers
- Letterheads
- Logos
- Newsletters
- Posters

To open a Theme Layout template:

1 In the **Startup Wizard**, in the **Create** section click **Use Design Template**.

2 In the **Choose a Design Template** dialog:

   • Select **Theme Layouts**.

   • Choose a theme layout category and then select a theme from the list.

   • In the adjacent pane, click a thumbnail to select a document type.

   • In the upper-right drop-down list, choose a document colour scheme (you can always change your mind later).

   • In the rightmost pane, select the pages to include in the layout.

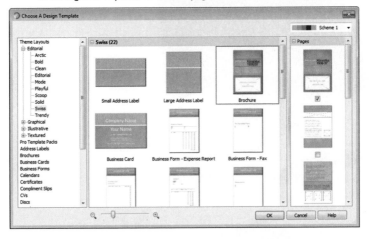

   • Click **OK**. The layouts are added as pages to your new publication.

The following pages provide previews of the **Theme Layout** templates provided with **PagePlus X5**.

Theme Layout: Arctic

- Brochure
- Letterhead
- Compliment Slip
- Business Cards
- Address Labels

Business Forms

- Expense Report
- Memorandum
- Fax Transmittal

- Inventory List
- Invoice
- Time Billing

- Quotation
- Purchase Order

... and more »

- Posters

- Newsletter
- Envelopes
- Flyers

Theme Layout: Bold

- Brochure
- Letterhead
- Compliment Slip
- Business Cards
- Address Labels

Business Forms

- Expense Report
- Memorandum
- Fax Transmittal
- Inventory List
- Invoice
- Time Billing
- Quotation
- Purchase Order

... and more »

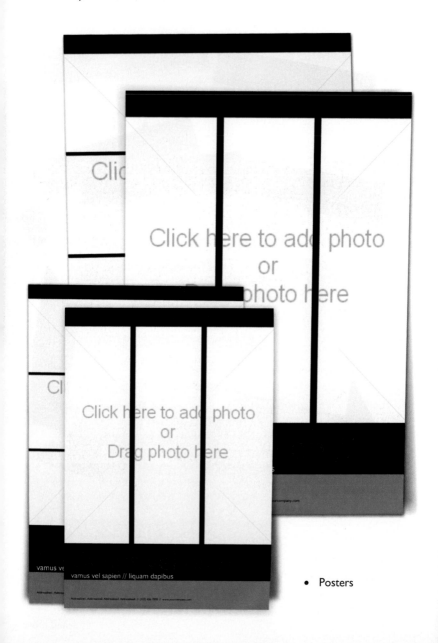

- Posters

- Newsletter
- Envelopes
- Flyers

Theme Layout: Clean

- Brochure
- Letterhead
- Compliment Slip
- Business Cards
- Address Labels

Business Forms

- Expense Report
- Memorandum
- Fax Transmittal

- Inventory List
- Invoice
- Time Billing

- Quotation
- Purchase Order

... and more »

- Posters

- Newsletter
- Envelopes
- Flyers

Theme Layout: Editorial

- Brochure
- Letterhead
- Compliment Slip
- Business Cards
- Address Labels

Business Forms

- Expense Report
- Memorandum
- Fax Transmittal
- Inventory List
- Invoice
- Time Billing
- Quotation
- Purchase Order

... and more »

- Posters

- Newsletter
- Envelopes
- Flyers

Theme Layout: Mode

- Brochure
- Letterhead
- Compliment Slip
- Business Cards
- Address Labels

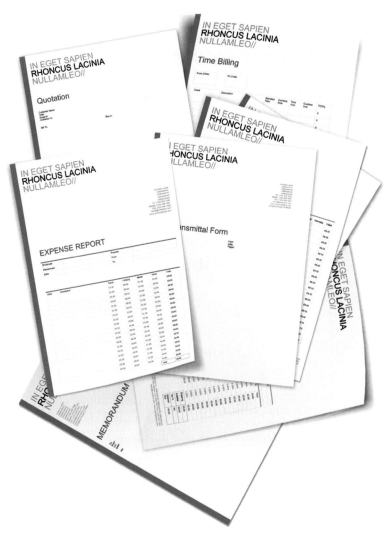

Business Forms

- Expense Report
- Memorandum
- Fax Transmittal
- Inventory List
- Invoice
- Time Billing
- Quotation
- Purchase Order

... and more »

IN EGET SAPIEN
RHONCUS LACINIA
NULLAMLEO//

Lorem ipsum dolor
Cras gravida sem
dui. Sed interdum,
porta massa, sed
Vestibulum ante i
ultrices posuere
metus. Nullam tin
ultrices ligula. In

Click here to add photo
or
Drag photo here

IN EGET SAPIEN
RHONCUS LACINIA
NULLAMLEO//

IN EGET SAPIEN
RHO
NUL

Lorem ipsum
Cras gravida s
dui. Sed interc
porta massa,
Vestibulum an
ultrices posue
metus. Nullam
ultrices ligula.

Click here to add photo
or
Drag photo here

r adipiscing elit. Cras gravida sem ut massa. Quisque
quat tristique, lacus nulla porta massa, sed
um primis in faucibus orci luctus et ultrices
. Nullam tincidunt posuere ligula. Aenean
are non, vestibulum ut, tempor porttitor, est.
urna convallis eleifend. Nulla feugiat eros at
sum vel dolor. Sed pulvinar. Etiam velit orci,
onec in odio sed nisl venenatis feugiat. •

(123) 456 7890

IN EGET SAPIEN
RHONCUS LACINIA
NULLAMLEO//

Lorem ipsum dolor sit amet, consectetuer adipiscing elit. Cras gravida sem ut massa. Quisque
accumsan porttitor dui. Sed interdum, nisl ut consequat tristique, lacus nulla porta massa, sed
imperdiet sem nunc vitae eros. Vestibulum ante ipsum primis in faucibus orci luctus et ultrices
posuere cubilia Curae; Pellentesque sit amet metus. Nullam tincidunt posuere ligula. Aenean
volutpat ultrices ligula. Suspendisse sem lorem, ornare non, vestibulum ut, tempor porttitor, est.
Quisque convallis aliquet eros. Nunc nec nulla eget urna convallis eleifend. Nulla feugiat eros at
augue. Integer feugiat nisi vitae velit. Cras cursus ipsum vel dolor. Sed pulvinar. Etiam velit orci,
pellentesque at, porttitor blandit, luctus eu, justo. Donec in odio sed nisl venenatis feugiat. •

(123) 456 7890

add photo

to here

Click here to add photo
or
Drag photo here

• Posters

- Newsletter
- Envelopes
- Flyers

Theme Layout: Playful

- Brochure
- Letterhead
- Compliment Slip
- Business Cards
- Address Labels

Business Forms

- Expense Report
- Memorandum
- Fax Transmittal
- Inventory List
- Invoice
- Time Billing
- Quotation
- Purchase Order

... and more »

- Posters

- Newsletter
- Envelopes
- Flyers

Theme Layout: Scoop

- Brochure
- Letterhead
- Compliment Slip
- Business Cards
- Address Labels

Business Forms

- Expense Report
- Memorandum
- Fax Transmittal
- Inventory List
- Invoice
- Time Billing
- Quotation
- Purchase Order

... and more »

Aliquam
Morbi nisl eros malesuada tempus!
Click here to add photo
or
Aliquam
Morbi nisl eros malesuada tempus!
Click here to add photo
or
Drag photo here
www.yourcompany.com
Mauris purus. Donec est nunc ornare non aliquet non tempus vel, dolor. Integer sapien nibh egestas ut!

- Posters

- Newsletter
- Envelopes
- Flyers

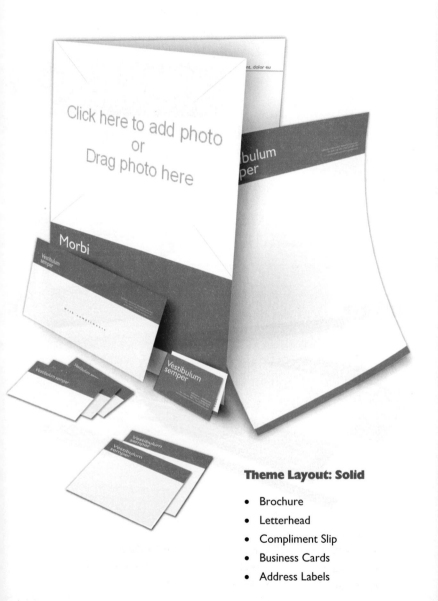

Theme Layout: Solid

- Brochure
- Letterhead
- Compliment Slip
- Business Cards
- Address Labels

Business Forms

- Expense Report
- Memorandum
- Fax Transmittal
- Inventory List
- Invoice
- Time Billing
- Quotation
- Purchase Order

... and more »

- Posters

- Newsletter
- Envelopes
- Flyers

Theme Layout: Swiss

- Brochure
- Letterhead
- Compliment Slip
- Business Cards
- Address Labels

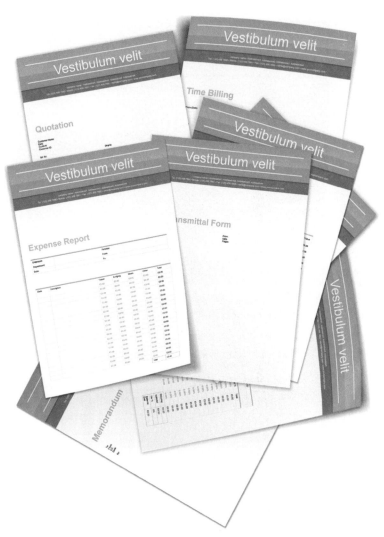

Business Forms

- Expense Report
- Memorandum
- Fax Transmittal
- Inventory List
- Invoice
- Time Billing
- Quotation
- Purchase Order

... and more »

- Posters

- Newsletter
- Envelopes
- Flyers

Theme Layout: Trendy

- Brochure
- Letterhead
- Compliment Slip
- Business Cards
- Address Labels

Business Forms

- Expense Report
- Memorandum
- Fax Transmittal
- Inventory List
- Invoice
- Time Billing
- Quotation
- Purchase Order

... and more »

- Posters

- Newsletter
- Envelopes
- Flyers

Theme Layout: Active

- Brochure
- Letterhead
- Compliment Slip
- Business Cards
- Address Labels

Business Forms

- Expense Report
- Memorandum
- Fax Transmittal

- Inventory List
- Invoice
- Time Billing

- Quotation
- Purchase Order

... and more »

- Posters

- Newsletter
- Envelopes
- Flyers

Theme Layout: Beta

- Brochure
- Letterhead
- Compliment Slip
- Business Cards
- Address Labels

Business Forms

- Expense Report
- Memorandum
- Fax Transmittal
- Inventory List
- Invoice
- Time Billing
- Quotation
- Purchase Order

... and more »

- Posters

- Newsletter
- Envelopes
- Flyers

Theme Layout: Curves

- Brochure
- Letterhead
- Compliment Slip
- Business Cards
- Address Labels

Business Forms

- Expense Report
- Memorandum
- Fax Transmittal
- Inventory List
- Invoice
- Time Billing
- Quotation
- Purchase Order

... and more »

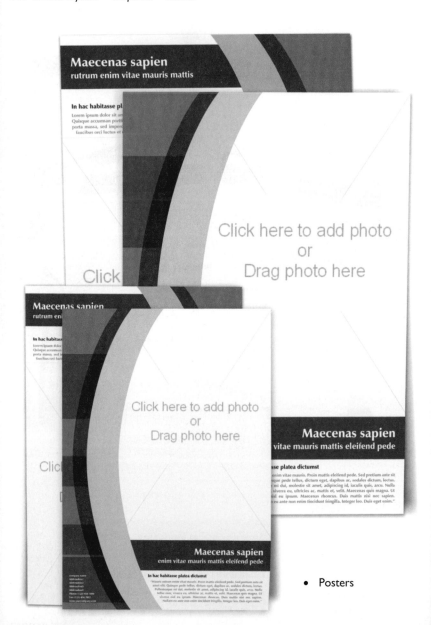

• Posters

- Newsletter
- Envelopes
- Flyers

Theme Layout: Decor

- Brochure
- Letterhead
- Compliment Slip
- Business Cards
- Address Labels

Business Forms

- Expense Report
- Memorandum
- Fax Transmittal

- Inventory List
- Invoice
- Time Billing

- Quotation
- Purchase Order

... and more »

- Posters

- Newsletter
- Envelopes
- Flyers

Theme Layout: Healthy

- Brochure
- Letterhead
- Compliment Slip
- Business Cards
- Address Labels

Business Forms

- Expense Report
- Memorandum
- Fax Transmittal

- Inventory List
- Invoice
- Time Billing

- Quotation
- Purchase Order

... and more »

- Posters

- Newsletter
- Envelopes
- Flyers

Theme Layout: Natural

- Brochure
- Letterhead
- Compliment Slip
- Business Cards
- Address Labels

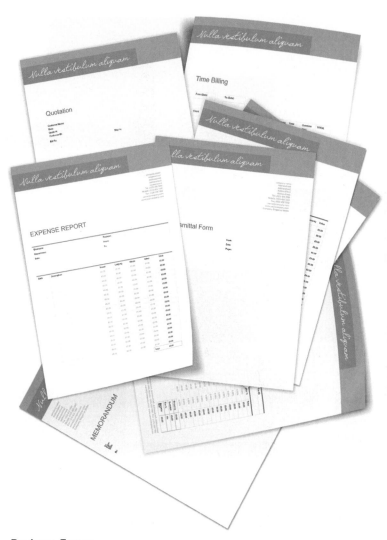

Business Forms

- Expense Report
- Memorandum
- Fax Transmittal
- Inventory List
- Invoice
- Time Billing
- Quotation
- Purchase Order

... and more »

• Posters

- Newsletter
- Envelopes
- Flyers

Theme Layout: Squares

- Brochure
- Letterhead
- Compliment Slip
- Business Cards
- Address Labels

Business Forms

- Expense Report
- Memorandum
- Fax Transmittal

- Inventory List
- Invoice
- Time Billing

- Quotation
- Purchase Order

... and more »

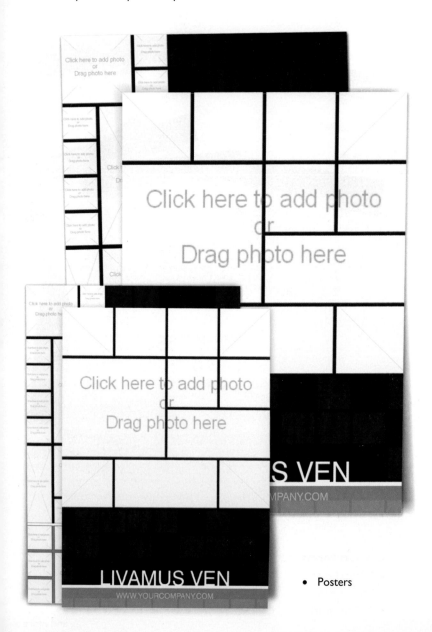

- Posters

- Newsletter
- Envelopes
- Flyers

Theme Layout: Supple

- Brochure
- Letterhead
- Compliment Slip
- Business Cards
- Address Labels

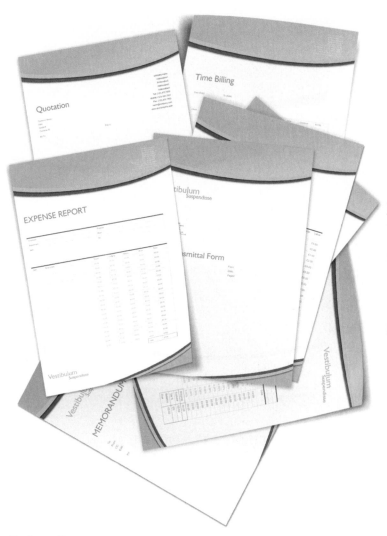

Business Forms

- Expense Report
- Memorandum
- Fax Transmittal

- Inventory List
- Invoice
- Time Billing

- Quotation
- Purchase Order

... and more »

- Posters

- Newsletter
- Envelopes
- Flyers

Theme Layout: Sylvan

- Brochure
- Letterhead
- Compliment Slip
- Business Cards
- Address Labels

Business Forms

- Expense Report
- Memorandum
- Fax Transmittal

- Inventory List
- Invoice
- Time Billing

- Quotation
- Purchase Order

... and more »

- Posters

- Newsletter
- Envelopes
- Flyers

Theme Layout: Tabs

- Brochure
- Letterhead
- Compliment Slip
- Business Cards
- Address Labels

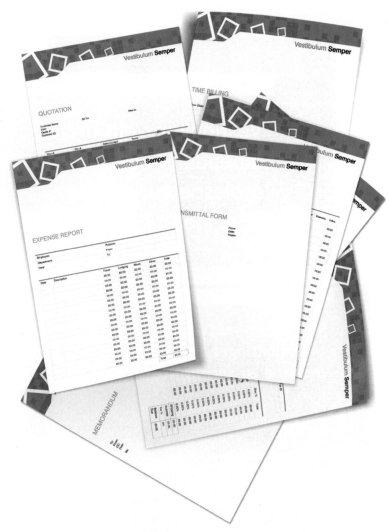

Business Forms

- Expense Report
- Memorandum
- Fax Transmittal
- Inventory List
- Invoice
- Time Billing
- Quotation
- Purchase Order

... and more »

- Posters

- Newsletter
- Envelopes
- Flyers

Theme Layout: Waveform

- Brochure
- Letterhead
- Compliment Slip
- Business Cards
- Address Labels

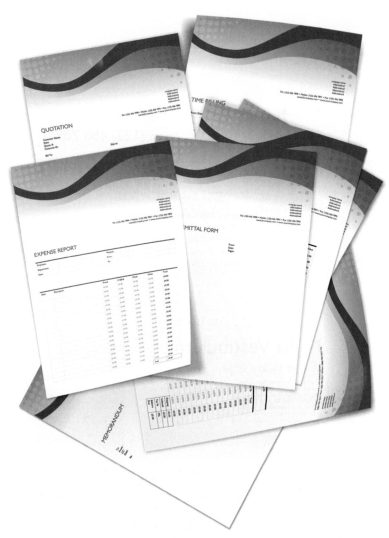

Business Forms

- Expense Report
- Memorandum
- Fax Transmittal
- Inventory List
- Invoice
- Time Billing
- Quotation
- Purchase Order

... and more »

(123) 456 7890

Nulla Vestibulum

In eget sapien vitae

Aliquam dapibus ipsum vitae sem.
Ut eget mauris ac nunc luctus
ornare. Phasellus enim augue,
rutrum tempus, blandit in,
vehicula eu, neque.

(123) 456 7890

Nulla Vestibulum

In eget sapien vitae

Aliquam dapibus ipsum vitae sem. Ut eget
mauris ac nunc luctus ornare. Phasellus enim
augue, rutrum tempus, blandit in, vehicula eu,
neque. Sed consequat nunc. Proin metus. Duis
at mi non tellus malesuada tincidunt. Cras in
neque. Sed lacinia, felis ut sodales pretium, justo
sapien hendrerit est, et convallis nisi quam sit
amet

- Posters

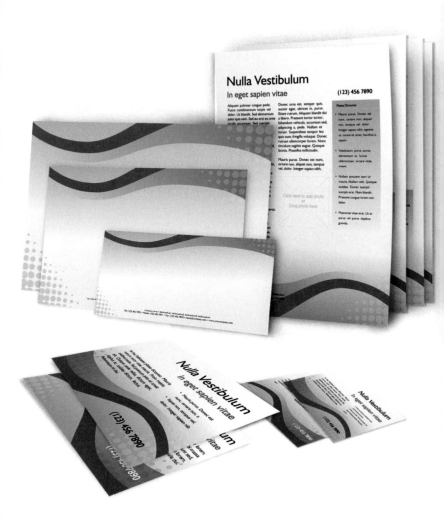

- Newsletter
- Envelopes
- Flyers

Theme Layout: Well Being

- Brochure
- Letterhead
- Compliment Slip
- Business Cards
- Address Labels

Business Forms

- Expense Report
- Memorandum
- Fax Transmittal
- Inventory List
- Invoice
- Time Billing
- Quotation
- Purchase Order

... and more »

• Posters

- Newsletter
- Envelopes
- Flyers

Theme Layout: Boxes

- Brochure
- Letterhead
- Compliment Slip
- Business Cards
- Address Labels

Business Forms

- Expense Report
- Memorandum
- Fax Transmittal

- Inventory List
- Invoice
- Time Billing

- Quotation
- Purchase Order

... and more »

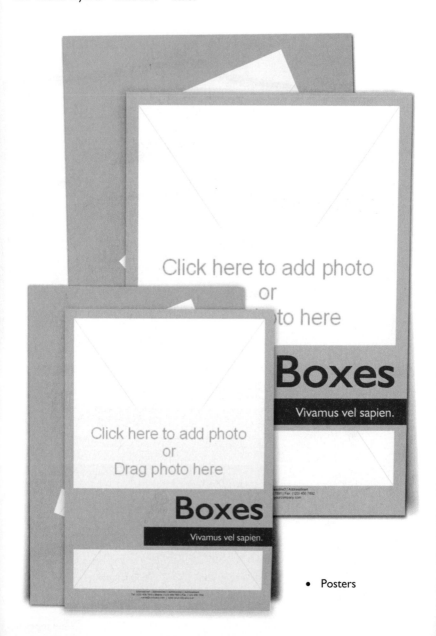

- Posters

- Newsletter
- Envelopes
- Flyers

Theme Layout: City

- Brochure
- Letterhead
- Compliment Slip
- Business Cards
- Address Labels

Business Forms

- Expense Report
- Memorandum
- Fax Transmittal
- Inventory List
- Invoice
- Time Billing
- Quotation
- Purchase Order

... and more »

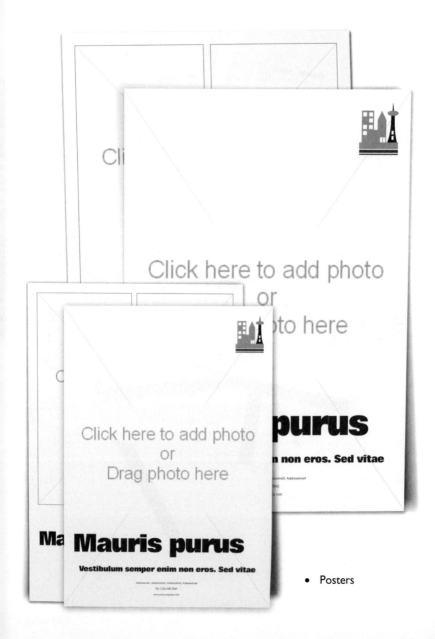

• Posters

- Newsletter
- Envelopes
- Flyers

Theme Layout: Globes

- Brochure
- Letterhead
- Compliment Slip
- Business Cards
- Address Labels

Business Forms

- Expense Report
- Memorandum
- Fax Transmittal
- Inventory List
- Invoice
- Time Billing
- Quotation
- Purchase Order

... and more »

- Posters

- Newsletter
- Envelopes
- Flyers

Theme Layout: Lines

- Brochure
- Letterhead
- Compliment Slip
- Business Cards
- Address Labels

Business Forms

- Expense Report
- Memorandum
- Fax Transmittal
- Inventory List
- Invoice
- Time Billing
- Quotation
- Purchase Order

... and more »

- Posters

- Newsletter
- Envelopes
- Flyers

Theme Layout: Spiro

- Brochure
- Letterhead
- Compliment Slip
- Business Cards
- Address Labels

Business Forms

- Expense Report
- Memorandum
- Fax Transmittal
- Inventory List
- Invoice
- Time Billing
- Quotation
- Purchase Order

... and more »

- Posters

- Newsletter
- Envelopes
- Flyers

Theme Layout: Tickle

- Brochure
- Letterhead
- Compliment Slip
- Business Cards
- Address Labels

Business Forms

- Expense Report
- Memorandum
- Fax Transmittal
- Inventory List
- Invoice
- Time Billing
- Quotation
- Purchase Order

... and more »

- Posters

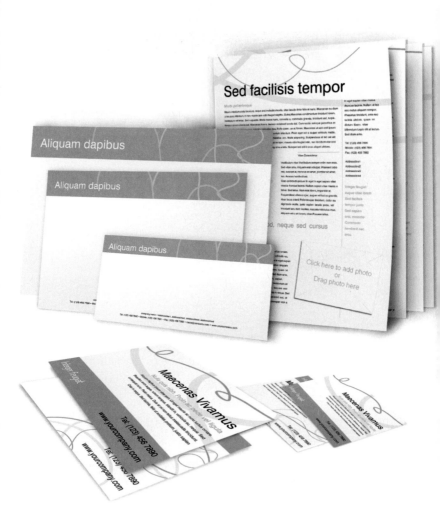

- Newsletter
- Envelopes
- Flyers

Theme Layout: Clouds

- Brochure
- Letterhead
- Compliment Slip
- Business Cards
- Address Labels

Business Forms

- Expense Report
- Memorandum
- Fax Transmittal
- Inventory List
- Invoice
- Time Billing
- Quotation
- Purchase Order

... and more »

- Posters

- Newsletter
- Envelopes
- Flyers

Theme Layout: Doodle

- Brochure
- Letterhead
- Compliment Slip
- Business Cards
- Address Labels

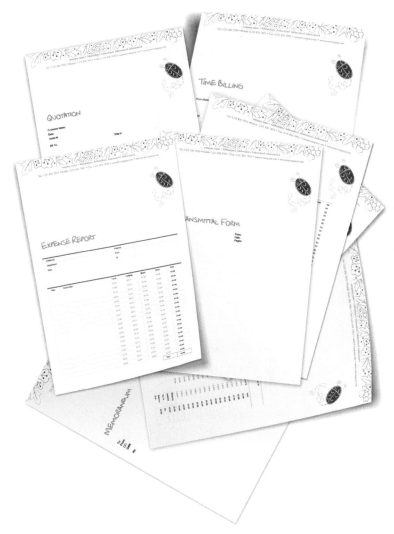

Business Forms

- Expense Report
- Memorandum
- Fax Transmittal
- Inventory List
- Invoice
- Time Billing
- Quotation
- Purchase Order

... and more »

- Posters

- Newsletter
- Envelopes
- Flyers

Theme Layout: Eco

- Brochure
- Letterhead
- Compliment Slip
- Business Cards
- Address Labels

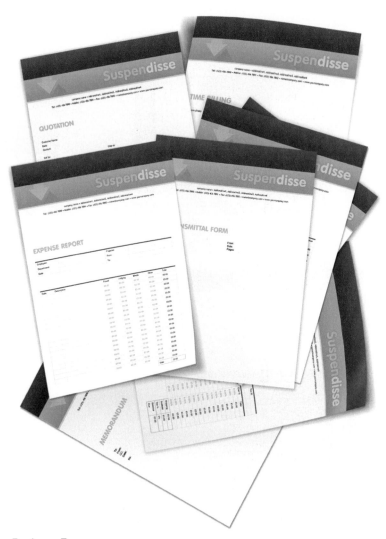

Business Forms

- Expense Report
- Memorandum
- Fax Transmittal
- Inventory List
- Invoice
- Time Billing
- Quotation
- Purchase Order

... and more »

- Posters

- Newsletter
- Envelopes
- Flyers

Theme Layout: Good

- Brochure
- Letterhead
- Compliment Slip
- Business Cards
- Address Labels

Business Forms

- Expense Report
- Memorandum
- Fax Transmittal
- Inventory List
- Invoice
- Time Billing
- Quotation
- Purchase Order

... and more »

- Posters

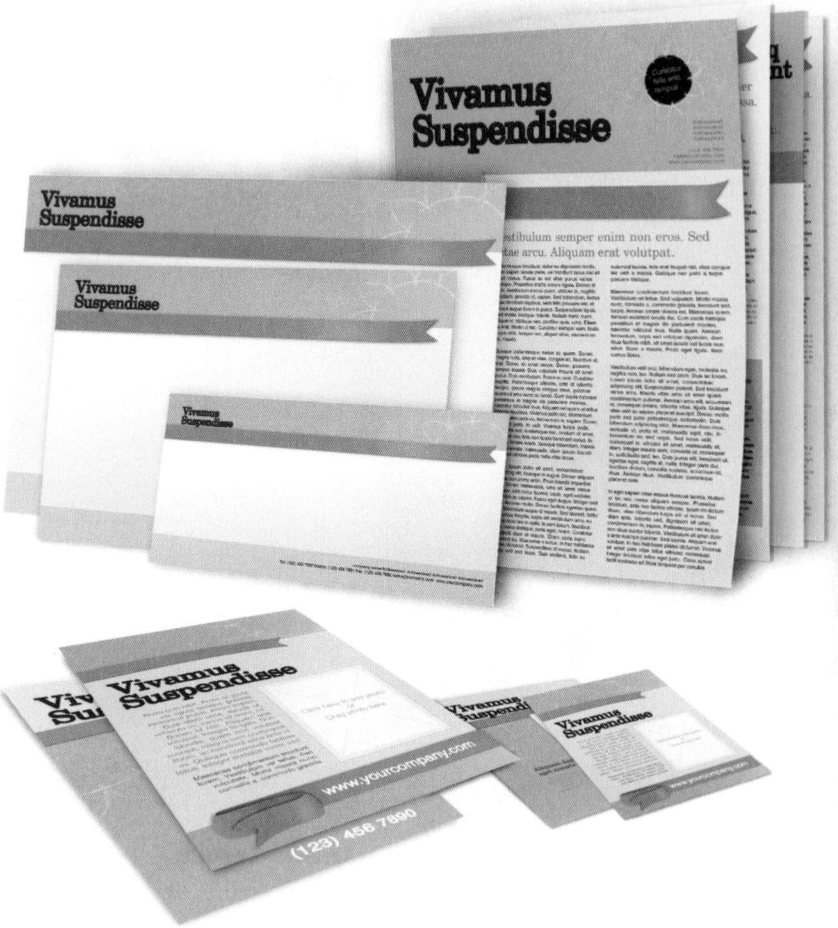

- Newsletter
- Envelopes
- Flyers

Theme Layout:

- Brochure
- Letterhead
- Compliment Slip
- Business Cards
- Address Labels

Business Forms

- Expense Report
- Memorandum
- Fax Transmittal
- Inventory List
- Invoice
- Time Billing
- Quotation
- Purchase Order

... and more »

- Posters

- Newsletter
- Envelopes
- Flyers

Theme Layout: Ledger

- Brochure
- Letterhead
- Compliment Slip
- Business Cards
- Address Labels

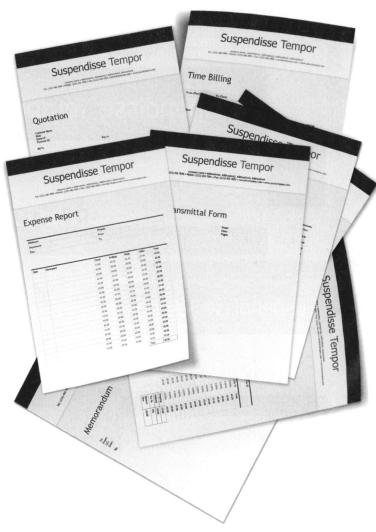

Business Forms

- Expense Report
- Memorandum
- Fax Transmittal
- Inventory List
- Invoice
- Time Billing
- Quotation
- Purchase Order

... and more »

- Posters

- Newsletter
- Envelopes
- Flyers

Theme Layout: Nature

- Brochure
- Letterhead
- Compliment Slip
- Business Cards
- Address Labels

Business Forms

- Expense Report
- Memorandum
- Fax Transmittal
- Inventory List
- Invoice
- Time Billing
- Quotation
- Purchase Order

... and more »

- Posters

- Newsletter
- Envelopes
- Flyers

Theme Layout: Paper

- Brochure
- Letterhead
- Compliment Slip
- Business Cards
- Address Labels

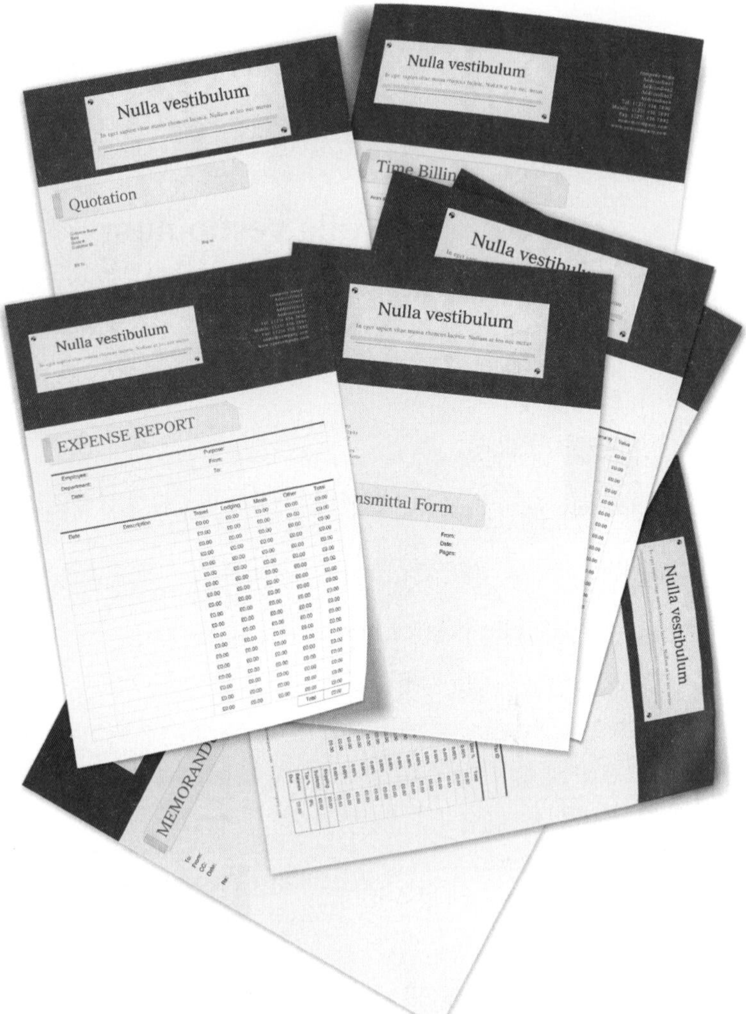

Business Forms

- Expense Report
- Memorandum
- Fax Transmittal
- Inventory List
- Invoice
- Time Billing
- Quotation
- Purchase Order

... and more »

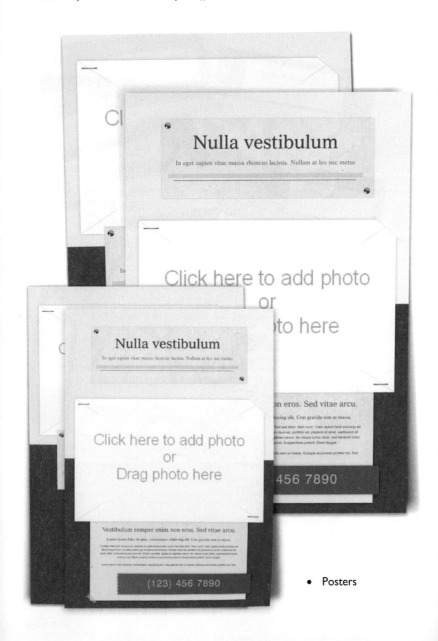

- Posters

- Newsletter
- Envelopes
- Flyers

Theme Layout: Pop

- Brochure
- Letterhead
- Compliment Slip
- Business Cards
- Address Labels

Business Forms

- Expense Report
- Memorandum
- Fax Transmittal

- Inventory List
- Invoice
- Time Billing

- Quotation
- Purchase Order

... and more »

- Posters

- Newsletter
- Envelopes
- Flyers

Theme Layout: Shabby

- Brochure
- Letterhead
- Compliment Slip
- Business Cards
- Address Labels

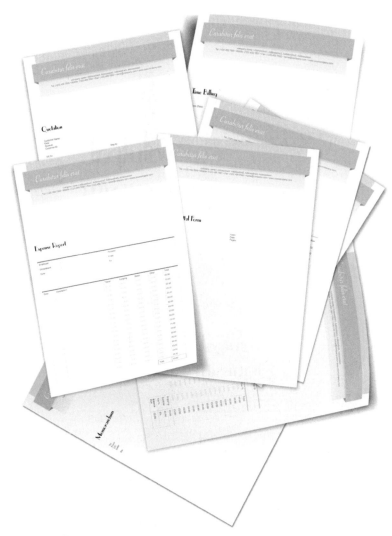

Business Forms

- Expense Report
- Memorandum
- Fax Transmittal
- Inventory List
- Invoice
- Time Billing
- Quotation
- Purchase Order

... and more »

- Posters

- Newsletter
- Envelopes
- Flyers

Theme Layout: Vintage

- Brochure
- Letterhead
- Compliment Slip
- Business Cards
- Address Labels

Business Forms

- Expense Report
- Memorandum
- Fax Transmittal
- Inventory List
- Invoice
- Time Billing
- Quotation
- Purchase Order

... and more »

- Posters

- Newsletter
- Envelopes
- Flyers

Theme Layout: Zine

- Brochure
- Letterhead
- Compliment Slip
- Business Cards
- Address Labels

Business Forms

- Expense Report
- Memorandum
- Fax Transmittal
- Inventory List
- Invoice
- Time Billing
- Quotation
- Purchase Order

... and more »

- Posters

- Newsletter
- Envelopes
- Flyers

3 Pro Template Packs

Pro Template Packs

PagePlus provides a selection of **Pro Template Pack** templates that you can use as starting points for your own publications.

These templates provide a wide range of document types. Each themed pack may contain the following categories:

- Brochures
- Business Cards
- Compliment Slips
- Emails
- Envelopes
- Flyers
- Letterheads
- Logos
- Menus
- Newsletters
- Posters
- Websites

To open a Pro Template Pack template:

1 In the **Startup Wizard**, in the **Create** section, click **Use Design Template**.

2 In the dialog, click to expand the **Pro Template Packs** category and then expand the **PagePlus X5** sub-category.

3 Select a 'theme' from the list and then select the template you want to use in the centre pane.

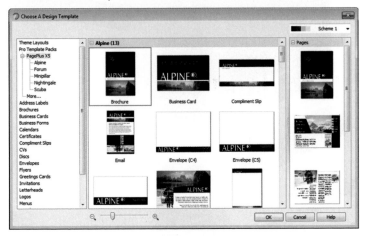

4 Click **OK** to open selected the template.

> For more information about **Design Templates**, see *Creating a publication from design templates* in PagePlus Help.

The following pages provide previews of the **Pro Template Packs** templates provided with **PagePlus X5**.

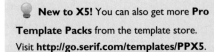

> **New to X5!** You can also get more **Pro Template Packs** from the template store. Visit **http://go.serif.com/templates/PPX5**.

Pro Template Pack: Alpine

- Brochure
- Business Card
- Compliment Slip
- Letterhead

- Envelopes
- Flyer
- Logo
- Newsletter
- Poster

... and more »

- Email
- Website

Pro Template Pack: Forum

- Brochure
- Business Card
- Compliment Slip
- Letterhead

... and more »

- Envelopes
- Flyer
- Logo
- Newsletter
- Poster

- Email
- Website

Pro Template Pack: Minipillar

- Brochure
- Business Card
- Compliment Slip
- Letterhead

- Envelopes
- Flyer
- Logo
- Newsletter
- Poster

... and more »

- Email
- Website

Pro Template Pack: Nightingale

- Brochure
- Business Card
- Compliment Slip
- Letterhead

... and more »

- Envelopes
- Flyer
- Logo
- Newsletter
- Poster